WHAT'S WHAT AND WHAT TO DO ABOUT IT

WHAT'S WHAT AND WHAT TO DO ABOUT IT

ANSWERS YOU DIDN'T KNOW YOU WANTED TO QUESTIONS YOU DIDN'T KNOW YOU HAD

WALDO MELLON

SEVEN STORIES PRESS
NEW YORK • OAKLAND • LONDON

Seven Stories Press
140 Watt Street
New York, NY 10013
www.sevenstories.com

Library of Congress Cataloging-in-Publication Data

Names: Mellon, Waldo, author.
Title: What's what and what to do about it : (answers you didn't know you wanted to questions you didn't know you had) / Waldo Mellon.
Description: New York, NY : Seven Stories Press, [2021]
Identifiers: LCCN 2021016202 (print) | LCCN 2021016203 (ebook) | ISBN 9781644210383 (hardcover) | ISBN 9781644210390 (ebook)
Subjects: LCSH: Conduct of life--Miscellanea.
Classification: LCC BJ1589 .M4624 2021 (print) | LCC BJ1589 (ebook) | DDC 170/.44--dc23
LC record available at https://lccn.loc.gov/2021016202
LC ebook record available at https://lccn.loc.gov/2021016203

Book design by Jon Gilbert

Printed in the USA.

9 8 7 6 5 4 3 2 1

For Allie and Jim.
Hi Mom. Hi Dad.

For Fred Finch
A Lovely Surprise
A Seed Spreader

[illegible]
(aka Waldo Mellon

Contents

THANKS A MILLION

Thanks a million to Jeannie and Jill Palmer and Micha Archer and Jimbo and Tiger and Peter and Bob Saul and Katie Shults and Bob Sturges and Denis O'Neill and Larry David and Nanny Vonnegut and Bruce Watson and Dick Metafora and Marc Berman and Ellen Moore and Barbara D'Arthenay and Lillian Pickering. For what? C'mon. You know for what.

Waldo Mellon's Fabulous Guarantee

Dear Reader,

My name is Waldo Mellon, and I cannot tell you how pleased I am that you are reading this. I know that there are lots of other things you could be doing at this moment, and for you to be passing your eyeballs over these particular words, of all the billions and billions of words there are to pass your eyeballs over, strikes me as nearly miraculous.

Not as miraculous, however, as the astounding acrobatics your brain is pulling off at this moment during the act of reading itself.

Reading is hard.

Reading well is harder.

And so I would like to make a special request. Please read this over a period of time, in short bursts. Ideally, you would read this only while sitting on the john. In most instances, the amount of time it would take you to complete your time on the john would be around the amount of time it would take you to read a single entry.

Here, in a nutshell, is my Main Idea: Life is a lovely, complicated accident. Our sweet little miraculous brains just do not have what it takes to understand it.

And so, in order to find enjoyment in our brief time exploring, we must simplify.

This book is my attempt at simplifying the complex.

I have no special training.

My guesses are no better than yours.

But I have written my guesses down and have wrestled them into a certain shape that I hope you may find helpful.

In fact, I am so hopeful that my guesses will be helpful to you that I am prepared to offer you . . .

WALDO MELLON'S FABULOUS GUARANTEE!

Here it is:

If you read the entire book, I guarantee that your life will begin to change for the better.

You will like yourself more.

You will be more relaxed.

You will anguish less over how you are perceived by others.

You will be better equipped to handle confusion and doubt.

You may still loathe yourself occasionally, and you may still feel blue and lost from time to time, and you may still be hounded by regret now and again. But those loud-mouthed young punks inside your head who have been tormenting you over the years will turn into toothless old farts waving to you from a bench in your skull.

You will see life in a slightly different way, and because of this you will spend more time feeling pleased and hopeful.

If none of this happens, then please, by all means, SEND AN EMAIL WITH YOUR ADDRESS TO:

WALDOMELLON1@GMAIL.COM

AND I, WALDO MELLON, SHALL SEND TO YOU, ON MY HONOR, A COMPLETE REFUND!!!

You heard me right. I am so confident that my version of things will improve your life that I am giving you a FABULOUS MONEY-BACK GUARANTEE!

Uh-oh. Could it be that my wife is right? That I have not thought this thing through? Hmmm . . .

A Brand-New Word

Before we get to the real heart of this book—to the letters—I want to introduce to you a brand-new word. This brand-new word is . . .

VOOCULE

Here's how it's pronounced: *Voo* rhymes with "boo." *Cule* rhymes with "mule." *Voocule*. Say it a few times. *Voocule*. *Voocule*. *Voocule*.

I'm hoping that the word will become as much a part of your vocabulary as the word "soul." Like your soul, your Voocule is a tough butterfly to net. It cannot be seen or touched or even located.

Every living thing has its own Voocule.

Plants included.

Your Voocule is your bubble. Your bubble of life.

What's inside?

YOU

The totality of you.

Every experience you have ever had.

Every thought.

Every dream.

Everything remembered.

Everything forgotten.

Everything hidden in the dark of your subconscious.

Everything you hate about yourself.

Everything you love about yourself.

And here's a very interesting fact: Every Voocule is exactly the same size. The Voocule of a baby mouse is no smaller than the Voocule of, say, Gandhi. Or an oak tree. Or Elvis.

How about that?!

And get this: You and only you can see what is inside your Voocule.

Do you see what this means? It means that you cannot see what is inside anyone else's bubble.

Which means that no living thing can see what is outside its own Voocule.

Which means that all living things exist in separate Voocules, an infinite and miraculous flotilla of wondrous magical bubbles that can enter each other but must always remain separate.

Which means . . . oh dear . . . every living thing is sealed in its own Voocule, isolated and forever alone . . .

Hmmm. I'm sensing that the fabulousness of my ground-breaking concept might not, at the moment, be making itself evident.

And so I'm going to sit you side by side on a park bench in a busy city with a loved one of your choosing. Neither one of you sees what the other sees.

Ever.

You both look at a portly fellow passing in a trench coat.

You think, That guy looks like my uncle Gus.

Your loved one thinks, Trench coat. Pervert?

Your attention turns to a pigeon.

You think, Are pigeons to birds what beggars are to people?

Your loved one thinks, If my head did that every time I took a step I'd shoot myself.

A skateboarder skateboards by.

You think, I gotta get more exercise.

Your loved one thinks, Why isn't he wearing elbow pads?

And on and on.

No two living things ever—EVER—react with their senses to the same thing in exactly the same way. Because everything is received through the prism of You, and you're the only You there is.

Why does this matter?

If you think of yourself as sharing a single huge bubble with every living thing, and the whole bunch of you seeing the same things in pretty much the same way, then when you fail you may begin to feel a smallness in comparison to the others, which may lead you to believe that you are flawed and deficient. And once you accept this as so, you may begin to build a structure of defense and resentment against those who you think are better than you.

On the other hand, when you succeed, you may begin to feel a grandiosity, which may lead you to believe that you are superior. And once you accept that this is so, you may begin to build a structure of defense and resentment against those who you think are less than you.

HEY! WHADYA KNOW? THEY BOTH LEAD TO THE SAME THING!

YOU VERSUS THEM!

NO GOOD. NO DAMN GOOD. FLAT OUT NO DAMN GOOD.

But...

If you think of all living things as organisms imprisoned in their own private bubble, in their own hermetically sealed Voocule, you may begin to feel a softening. You may begin to feel a greater sense of a shared struggle to be understood.

A better understanding of our common loneliness, our common helplessness.

A recognition that we all bang our fists upon our own edges, wanting more.

That we are all desperate for a closeness we can never attain.

And this is at the heart of what people mean when they say that life is hard.

Getting people to truly understand you is impossible, because there is no window into this Voocule of yours where someone can suddenly see everything the way you see everything.

No one, but no one, can see what you see the way you see it.

And now, on to the letters in bottles that have been tossed to the seas and the sands from the flotilla of Voocules.

Brains

Dear Waldo,

I think I'm going nuts. Because sometimes I try to focus my brain and it won't focus. Or I'll have a great idea that gets me all excited and ten minutes later I can't remember it. Or I'll be sitting there and something will pop into my head, but I have absolutely no clue whatsoever where it came from. But even worse is sometimes I get the most horrible, horrible sick thoughts that I would never in a million years tell anybody. Is this normal or am I headed for the loony bin?

Thanks,
Edna Pfeiffer

Dear Edna,

All I can say is if you're going to the loony bin, reserve a double because I'm going there with you. My brain does all the things yours does. I don't worry, though, because I've come to know that my brain is not really mine. It's like a little pet that lives in the kennel of my head.

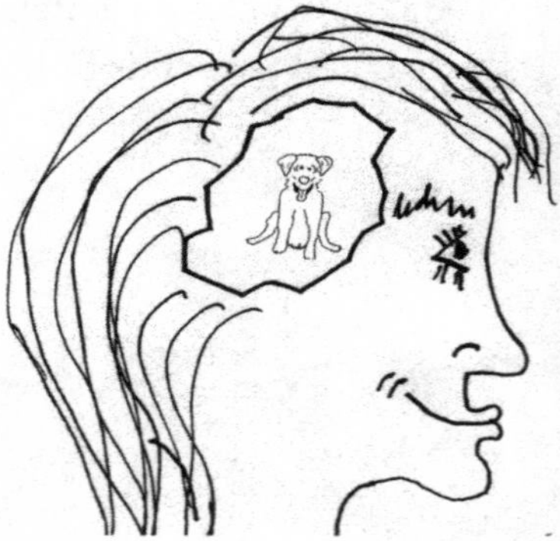

It's a bright little pooch, and I feel like I've taught it some pretty good tricks, but the damn thing is always dashing off into the bushes chasing who knows what and ending up lost.

Sometimes I'll call and call and call and my brain just sits there ignoring me. Other times it appears out of nowhere with the damnedest things in its mouth.

And so, Edna, in my opinion it's best to think of your brain as something separate from the rest of you, as an entertaining, unpredictable rascal that you're stuck with.

As you live your life, you will be making constant deposits into this brain of yours, but your brain will continue to treat you as if it's in the employ of a superior enemy.

It will taunt you with regrets. It will bathe paths you have not taken in a golden light. And it will airbrush memories of the past in such a way that your life now may seem dim and without luster by comparison.

But you must not get suckered in. It's just the little rascal in your head fooling around.

Thank you for your letter.

Your Fan,

Waldo Mellon

Genitals

Dear Waldo,

My problem has nothing to do with my big head. It has to do with my smaller head. The other day I walked into a video store with my two kids looking for a movie, and there was this life-sized cardboard cutout of a movie starlet. This particular life-sized cardboard cutout freezes the starlet in a pose in which she's walking away, looking seductively at the viewer—me—and beckoning him—me—with a curling finger to follow her. Her eyes followed me everywhere I went. I know this because I traveled each of the one hundred and eighty degrees in front of her flat face with the heat of her eyes burning directly into me. I imagined nibbling on her ear. I was wondering what it would be like to kiss lips that were that big and pouty when my kids arrived with their video choice, which was *Toy Story 2*.

Waldo, Jesus Christ, the thing was cardboard. Do I have a problem here?

Worried Dad

Dear Worried Dad,

Good news. No, you do not have a problem. Bad news. What you do have is genitals.

Genitals pee, yes, but that is not what they're really known for. What genitals are known for is sex. You are lucky enough to have been the result of the amazing chemical stunt called Life. But I'm afraid you have been saddled with the helpless compulsion to reproduce.

Unfortunately genitals, with the possible exception of the underside of the tongue, are visually the most disgusting part of the body that we get to see without stepping on a land mine.

Genitals, when you rub them in a certain way, I don't care who you are— Saint Peter, Santa Claus, Lady Gaga—you're going to make the kind of noises and behave in such a way that nobody is going to want to be around you for very long if you don't cut it out.

In the production of pleasure, genitals have no rival. Enlightenment packs a wallop but takes years and involves a lot of waiting. An orgasm, particularly for males, is quick, easy, and fun fun fun. The only time you're not crazy about having one is immediately after you've just had one.

And here's why this is so: It's simple math. If a living thing dies more often than it replaces itself, game over. Extinction. And so, after eons of trial and error, evolution has stumbled upon a fantastic, although somewhat obvious, simple trick for surviving if you aren't a plant:

MAKE REPRODUCING MORE FUN THAN
ABSOLUTELY ANYTHING ELSE

Worried Dad, have you ever seen a jumbo jet waiting to take off? If you look through the little window at the front, you might catch a glimpse of the captain. Doesn't the captain look tiny? Well, Cap'n Pee-Wee controls the entire gigantic object behind him.

Think of Cap'n Pee-Wee as your genitals. A small fraction of your total body that's often in charge of the rest of you and can

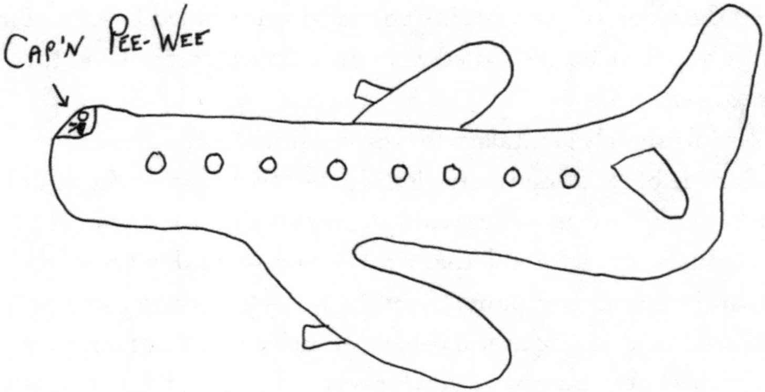

make you act like a fool. For example, my dog Tank, who doesn't even have any testicles, humps the arm of my couch, the leg of my wife, the suitcases of our guests. Bill Clinton, a brilliant man, just could not pass up having his genitals blown. Could not. Just could not. That's how much crazy, ridiculous fun it is. It's even more fun than being president.

Lusting after a cardboard likeness of a movie starlet, Worried Dad, is nothing but proof that you're a living thing that is not a plant.

By the way, did you guys like *Toy Story 2*? I sure did.

Your Fan,

Waldo Mellon

Stupidity

Dear Waldo,

I said the stupidest thing ever to this woman I think I might be in love with and now I'm afraid she must think I'm stupid. My question is, how do you know if you're stupid or not? Please, I don't want to be stupid.

Thanks,

Gretchen S.

Dear Gretchen S.,

I will bet you whatever you don't mind losing that I can outstupid you any day of the week. Get this: I'm twelve years old and my uncle, trying to make a point to a kitchen full of people about the sad state of education, asks me who fought in the Civil War.

Here's exactly what I say: North and South? So far, so good. But then I add, just in case: East and West? I can still feel the horrible blood-heat rising to my face as if I've bent over to sniff a hot radiator.

Here's another radiator-sniffer: I'm twenty-one, and my blind date tells me she's been reading Flannery O'Connor. She asks if I like Flannery O'Connor. Oh yes, says the college boy, I do, I like him very very much. Flannery O'Connor, I'm informed, is a she.

Gretchen, these are just for starters. Again and again, to avoid the hot-faced humiliation of not knowing, I've pretended to have heard of things I never heard of, claimed to have read things I never read, nodded great big of-course-of-course nods without a clue what everybody was talking about. For the longest time, Gretchen, the worst thing that could happen to me was that my Big Secret would be discovered: that I really was, all kidding aside, stupid.

And then my wonderful aunt Jane sends me a present for my thirty-sixth birthday: a framed passage, copied in elegant calligraphy, written by a man I had never heard of, Henry Beston:

> *We need another and a wiser and perhaps a more mystical concept of animals. Remote from universal nature and living by complicated artifice, man in civilization surveys the creature through the glass of his knowledge and sees thereby a feather magnified and the whole image in distortion. We patronize them for their incompleteness, for their tragic fate of having taken form so far below ourselves. And therein we err, and greatly err. For the animal shall not be measured by man. In a world older and more complete than ours, they move finished and complete, gifted with extensions of the senses we have lost or never attained, living by voices we shall never hear. They are not brethren, they are not underlings, they are other nations, caught with ourselves in the net of life and time, fellow prisoners of the splendor and the travail of the earth.*

And Gretchen, hallelujah! Suddenly I'm released! I'm free! Free to be stupid if that's what you want to call me. Because when I read that passage, in my guts, in my heart, there's no way I'm on the Civilized Man Team. No way.

I'm on the Animal Team.

I'm just one of the creatures who gets distorted when Civilized Man surveys me through the big fancy glass of his superior knowledge.

So are you. So is everybody. Henry Beston got a lot of things right, but he got one thing wrong: There is no Civilized Man team. There's only . . .

THE ANIMAL TEAM!

Okay, so maybe I'm a little shaky on the topic of the Civil War, but so are ducks. So are antelope. So are dolphins. So are june bugs. They're complete. I'm complete too. We just don't happen to know the same things.

We're all just animals making our best guesses about how to get through the day.

And this woman who may think you're stupid, Gretchen, all she's really saying is what anybody is saying when anybody calls somebody else stupid, which is: Well, looks like the two of us know different things.

If you're having a hard time thinking of yourself as just another animal, remember:

"We need another and a wiser and perhaps a more mystical concept of animals."

Yes we do, Henry Beston. Yes we do.

I hope you find something helpful in here, Gretchen. Thanks for your letter.

Your Fan,

Waldo Mellon

Beliefs

Dear Waldo:

I read with mounting disdain your letter to Gretchen S. in which you hypothesized, if I may use such a dignified word for your drivel, that human beings are simply one more life-form on a planet teeming with life-forms, as incomplete and as floundering as the rest of the lot.

I own homes in six different time zones. I can glance at any page in a telephone directory, close it, and then flawlessly recite the names in alphabetical order. My mind is sharp. I have made my money by studying how money is made, and then by making more money with money. Success in life depends not upon guessing well, but upon knowing, and then making choices with confidence based upon that knowledge. Both my values and what I know to be true are constant and non-negotiable. I am a beneficiary of the greatest idea on the face of the earth—capitalism—which rewards excellence, achieved by either hard work or genetic good fortune or both, and I will be damned if I'll stand by quietly when someone, even someone as minor as yourself, suggests that I and a june bug are equal miracles.

Anonymous

Dear Anonymous,

Thank you for your refreshingly direct letter. You are absolutely correct: I do think you and a june bug are equal miracles.

You say that success depends upon knowing. We differ on this, in that I think "knowing" is just another word for "I'm done thinking about it."

You say your values are constant. We differ on this too, in that I think values are a flimsy product of random circumstance.

In hopes of making my point, I'm inviting you to play a fabulous game I've devised called Which Would You Smack with a Shovel? The rules are simple: I'm going to give you an imaginary shovel and an imaginary table upon which I am going to place different sets of imaginary things.

Okay, Anonymous, here we go.

I'm now placing on the table a small grayish stone and a beautiful living butterfly.

Raise your shovel, please. And now bring it down hard upon one of them.

Good show, Anonymous. You've made it clear that you value Life and Beauty more than you value Non-Life and Grayishness.

Okay. Let's brush the bits of stone off the table. And next to the same beautiful butterfly, let's place another small stone much like the last one, but shaped, when viewed from a particular angle, like a lopsided heart. This stone belonged to your great-grandfather. It was given to him by your great-grandmother, who found it one clear summer day when they were courting, and until his death your great-grandfather kept that stone in the right front pocket of his trousers, rubbing it with his thumb whenever he needed soothing.

Okay. Raise your shovel, please, Anonymous, and bring it down hard upon just one imaginary object.

Eww. Sorry, butterfly. So much for Beauty and Life.

But hooray for Sentimental Value.

Okay. Let's sponge the residual dust of the beautiful butterfly off the table and replace it, next to your great-grandpa's stone, with another lump of stuff also found in the ground. It's a diamond. I have no idea how much it's worth.

Okay. Anonymous, raise your shovel. And now, please smack one of the two imaginary objects on the table.

I know you're a smart guy when it comes to money, Anonymous, and so I'm guessing that you brought the shovel down on your great-grandpa's stone just in case the diamond is worth a lot. And I have wonderful imaginary news for you: The imaginary diamond is real. In fact, it has been assessed by imaginary licensed gem brokers at over seven hundred and fifty thousand dollars!

Great going! Good judgment! You own that diamond now!

Okay. Now onto the table I'm placing your fabulous diamond and an imaginary mongrel dog donated by your local ASPCA. And under the drumroll of an imaginary professional drummer, please raise your shovel and do your thing!

Well, as we wrap the poor imaginary poochy in a sheet, I must deliver to you some disturbing news. The imaginary licensed gem brokers were crooks. They made off with the real diamond, and in its place put a chunk of well-cut glass.

I don't blame you, Anonymous, for hurling your imaginary shovel into the imaginary bushes.

You don't want to play anymore?

Who would? Soon you were going to have to make even harder choices: chimpanzee/panda bear, white baby/brown baby, beautiful-womanwho-despises-you/homely-woman-who-adores-you. And on and on.

The good news is, you're free to go. The bad news is, sorry, there's no way out of this game. Because in real life, every choice you make is based upon your values and your beliefs.

Anonymous, I admit that my silly game was rigged in my favor. And okay okay okay, I take it back, you're a slightly bigger miracle than a june bug. But I stick by my opinion that there's not a rug you're standing on that cannot be pulled out from under you, and that you're not nearly as big a shot as you think you are.

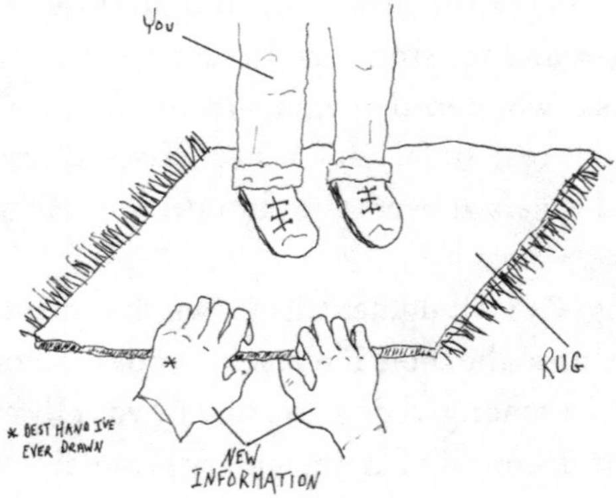

We might not ever be friends, but I'm still glad you wrote to me.

Your Fan,
Waldo Mellon

Breasts

Dear Waldo,

Your earlier endorsement of lusting after cardboard women has made my wife storm off, and so I am writing this letter alone in the dark. I am asking you for help in dealing with our only child, Joy, who is twelve.

According to Joy's teacher, Mrs. Hetterman, the boys in her sixth-grade class have noticed, as have we, that her mammary glands are beginning to develop to the extent that they are causing her blouse or sweater or even her art smock to push forward in a very visible manner, causing the boys to behave, in Mrs. Hetterman's words, like popcorn in a microwave.

Of course my wife and I understand that mammary glands are a natural part of every young girl's maturation process, and when I said those very words to Joy as part of my opening statement at our Sunday family meeting, Joy requested that we call them what the boys in her class call them, which is "titties." As neither my wife nor I felt comfortable calling them that, we cut our weekly meeting short and played Boggle.

Waldo, by next Sunday's meeting we want to be much better prepared, re: mammary glands. Can you offer some advice on how to handle this delicate and confusing topic?

Thank you in advance,

Ray and (in absentia) Suzanne

Dear Ray and (in absentia) Suzanne,

I do indeed have some advice. Every moment in life is both prose and poetry. Prose is what you are thinking. Poetry is what you are feeling. The reason you're so confused at the moment is because you're unsure if mammary glands, as you are calling them, are prose or poetry.

I'm with you. It's a tough one. For starters, nobody knows what to call them.

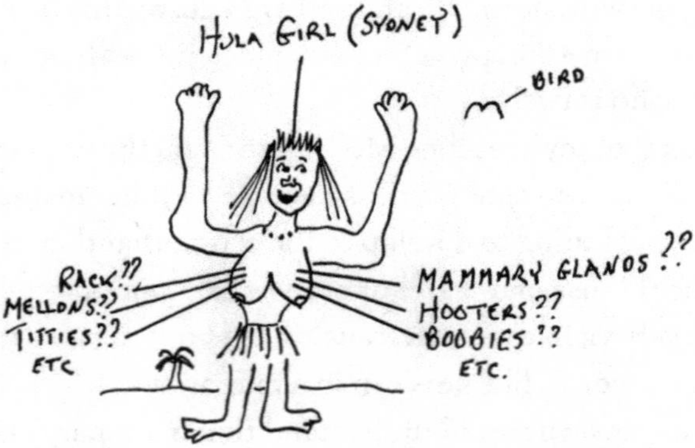

"Mammary glands," in my opinion, has an autopsy-ish ring to it that might set the wrong tone.

Similarly, honoring your daughter's request to refer to them as "titties" runs the risk of conjuring up a snack food, which may not be the best thing.

And I probably don't have to tell you to avoid the horrible Hooter clan, with their inbred cousins Rack and Boobies and Knockers and Headlights and Front Porch and so forth.

You may be tempted, for the sake of simple sweetness and innocence, to call them "bosoms" at your meeting. But for me, "bosoms" has always invoked that clown Bozo, a very fine clown but not an ideal reference point around which to wrap a delicate discussion.

And so, in spite of the poultry connection, I'm recommending that you use the term "breasts." Joy is developing breasts. "Jesus at his mother's breasts" just feels so much better to me than "Jesus at his mother's hooters."

On behalf of my gender, I feel helplessly apologetic for our behavior around breasts. Your sweet daughter, like every other woman whose breasts cast a shadow, shall soon be saddled with false advertising. She shall be sent out into the world with a sandwich board that broadcasts, through no doing of her own, "Sex! Sex! Come 'n get it! Sex!"

No, that is not what she wants. That is not what she is asking for. And that must be so wearisome.

What's to be done?

My advice, Ray and (in absentia) Suzanne, is to call them "breasts," and to talk in prose about them, and to talk in poetry about them. And in your talk I suggest you mention the loveliness of love, and the dangers of lust, and the mysteries of life, and how much you adore this human called Joy who is growing up. Breasts or no breasts, that will be time well spent.

Your Fan,

Waldo Mellon

Horrors

Dear Waldo,

Every time I open the papers or go online there's news of people doing horrible things. And I do mean horrible. Opening fire in movie theaters, throwing babies off bridges, eating somebody else's face off. I'm not perfect. Once I got so angry I slapped someone and I think it's made me what I am today, which is always sorry. For example, I make saltwater taffy and I give it out to almost anybody, hoping being nice might spread. I guess my question is, how can people do horrible things? How?

Sincerely,
Bertha

Dear Bertha,

When I was in my mid-twenties I found a little featherless pink baby bird in the street and I took that baby bird home and put it into a nest I made from a shoebox and Kleenex. I fed it earthworms and bread soaked in milk, and each time I did this I'd make little high-pitched noises, my version of Mama Noises so that it might think of me as its mother. Each time I did this, the tiny beak opened wide to the ceiling as if food fell like rain from the sky.

My airline-pilot brother came up with a great name for this bird: Whisperjet.

Each morning as I approached the nest, I expected Whisperjet to be dead, but no.

The feathers kept blooming like flowers, and soon the little pink thing declared itself to be a blue jay.

And in no time Whisperjet was flying about the house, shitting on couches, shitting on lampshades, shitting on the heads of guests.

The time had come to release Whisperjet into the wild.

I find him in the kitchen on the rim of a pot. I push my forefinger into his chest. He steps onto it.

I carry him outdoors.

Whisperjet looks up, cocks his head. Outdoors? Outdoors?

Oh yes, outdoors.

Whisperjet cocks one eye to me.

And then he's off.

And I follow him with my eyes until my little friend becomes too small to see.

Bye, Whisperjet. Bye.

Yay.

Freedom.

Whisperjet is free.

Yay.

Kind of yay.

Kind of not yay.

The next morning I discover some sweet bird shit I hadn't seen before on the toaster and find myself smiling.

I go outside. I look around.

Why not?—I make my Mama Noise.

I make my Mama Noises again and again.

And now I glimpse myself as a sad fool in a bad movie, standing in his yard in his underwear, chirping at the sky.

But then by god Whisperjet circles out of nowhere and lands on my head.

This is a fact. Word of honor. This happened.

And it happened again and again for months until the seasons changed, and cold nights arrived, and then Whisperjet did what blue jays do I guess, which is go somewhere else.

And so, Bertha, what this says to me is this: that we all begin as desperate and helpless pink things sitting in a busy road, waiting to be scooped up.

Anything that offers hope becomes something to cling to. Much of the time, if all goes well, our saviors are some version of our parents. For all to go well, however, we must feel wanted. If we are thought of as something burdensome, a nuisance interfering with greater pleasures, how easy it is then for our saviors to take our pink vulnerability and destroy us. To blame us for their self-loathing. To teach us never to trust, to never open our mouths wide to the great big blue sky

Whisperjet had to rewire himself again and again in order to think of my head as a safe haven to land upon.

All it took from me, though, was reliable, repeated, ordinary kindness.

If you ask me, it's as simple as this: treat new pink things with regular kindness and the world gets better.

And I do hope, Bertha, that you get to have some of your salt-water taffy sometimes, because you sound awfully nice to me. If I were a bird I would certainly land on your head.

Your Fan,

Waldo Mellon

Luck

Dear Waldo,

I hear you saying again and again that everything is just all in your fucking head. It's all in my head, is it? Please pay attention to this. I got one leg. I got no feet. I got a big welt on my cheek, plus no job, plus a cleft palate, plus a family of fleas climbing up my legs every time I piss in this so-called homeless shelter. How does telling me it's all in my fuckin head get me one cunt-hair closer to what you got?

Unsinfuckincerely,

One-legged footless jobless man etfuckincetera

Dear One-legged Footless Jobless Man
Etfuckincetera,

Although I wish you could have found another way of measuring progress, you ask a good and fair question. And I wish I knew your first name so I could use it to ease into the intimacy of what I'm about tell you.

I have been genetically handed a cellular malfunction called hemochromatosis. It's a glamourless, low-rent sleazebag of a disease, in that it spends lots of time just lurking. It lurked in me until I was in my forties, when it presented itself by turning the cartilage in a number of my joints into peanut brittle. My two knees and my two shoulders have been replaced by shiny new miracle fakes I'm grateful for. But I can't do lots of the things I used to love doing. I move differently. Sometimes my kids call me Tin Man.

On a good day when they call me Tin Man, I grin as I work to pick up the Frisbee, thinking, Lucky me to have healthy, funny children who like to laugh with their dad on this wonderful clear summer day. Lucky me to feel the sun and to love my wife and my home and my life. Lucky me to have all that I have.

On a bad day when they call me Tin Man, I grin as I work to pick up the Frisbee, thinking, Fuck you, you little rat-faced shits, and fucking A it's muggy and hot and let's see how you like getting old and go chase the fucking Frisbee because I just threw it into the thorn bushes, whadya think about that?!

See the difference?

On those two very different days, nothing outside my head has changed. The only thing that has changed is inside my head.

There are things you can fix and there are things that you cannot fix.

The things that you cannot fix, you have to sit with them and get to know them better. You have to accept them or you will live a bitter life.

You have to focus on the things that you can do. You have to locate pleasures and do what it takes to visit them often.

And please be patient.

I know you're wanting to tell me to go fuck myself, and I don't blame you. Tin Man is rooting for you.

Your Fan,

Waldo Mellon

Death

Dear Waldo,

I like it when you talk about death. See, I'm a long-distance truck driver, and my CB handle is 6 Feet Under because all I think about is death. The main thing I don't get is how if someone (God) has the skillset to create people, then how can that same someone (God) not just make it so you never kick the bucket ever?

The fact is I think about the horrible inky blackness of death morning noon and night. You happen to have any helpful tips on this particular topic?

Sincerely,
6 Feet Under

Dear 6 Feet Under,

I'm delighted to tell you that you're making the same blunder many, many people make. You're thinking of Death as something negative.

The fact is that nobody has the foggiest idea of what happens after Death. So this frees us from the ball and chain of logic. Which in turn releases two powerful forces:

FEAR AND IMAGINATION

This fantastic combo can result in sublime works of art but doesn't offer much in the way of packing tips for The Final Journey.

So what about this: I'm guessing, 6 Feet Under, that you have an appointment book of some sort in which you keep track of things you're supposed to do in the coming weeks or months.

But now I'm asking you to consider a very different kind of appointment book. This is an appointment book that I'm calling

YOUR ETERNAL APPOINTMENT BOOK

Your Eternal Appointment Book has an infinite number of pages. I'm asking you now to spend some time thumbing through them.

As you'll soon discover, most of the pages look identical. Your appointments for most of eternity really boil down to just a single obligation:

FLOAT AROUND

Go ahead. Leaf through the pages. Eon after eon after eon, just Floating Around.

However, on one of those infinite number of pages you will find this:

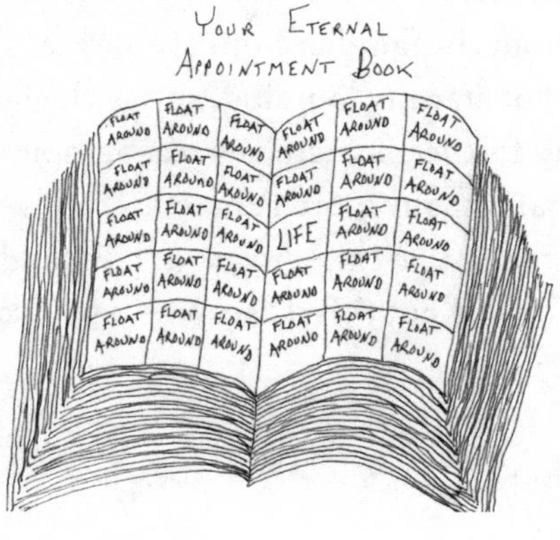

LIFE!

It may be very difficult to find because you're thumbing through eternity, but it's there, I promise you.

Because it's Your Life.

6 Feet Under, what if you think of Your Life as a Fabulous Holiday, a frisky time when you break away from the daily grind to do what you don't ordinarily do, go where you don't ordinarily go, drink drinks you don't ordinarily drink, wear hats you don't ordinarily wear.

Oh sure, every holiday includes its hardships and annoyances—lost luggage, sunburn, internal parasites—but the novelty and excitement more than make up for it. Holiday Time is a time to let loose.

And then, like all things, your Fabulous Holiday must come to an end.

And now you just come back Home.

I have to tell you I really like this configuration. It makes me sad to think about the end of my own Fabulous Holiday, but it doesn't make me worried or scared. Holidays are great fun, but after all the hullabaloo isn't there something calming—even appealing—about the familiar hum of routine?

And with all of eternity looming, and with all of your Stuff floating around forever, is there any reason not to believe that there will be many, many more Fabulous Holidays to come?

A good start might be changing your CB handle. Instead of 6 Feet Under, how about this: Dead My Ass! I like that. Hang in there, Dead My Ass.

Your Fan,

Waldo Mellon

God

Dear Waldo,

Your take on death really irks me and I'm going to tell you why. What's this "floating around" business? Saying we just "float around" when we die is a cop-out if I ever heard one. With something as huge as death, I want details. If you can't give me some good old-fashioned specifics then I'm going to stick with the heaven/angels/clouds option, which at least has some fancy gates to pass through, which is more than I can say for your vague "floating around" hogwash.

Signed,
No Pushover

Dear No Pushover,

Okay, I see you want to play hardball. Fine. I'm in. Let's get to it.

To help me clarify my position, I'd like to introduce you to My Filthy Bum Harvey, who at the moment is sleeping in the weeds beneath a tree at the edge of a park. I've known this destitute hobo for years and consider him a friend, so I don't think he'll mind us tippy-toeing up to him and using him to make a few points.

First, I'm going to lift the flaps of Harvey's lips in order to expose his teeth. In the light of my new laser pointer, which I've purchased especially for this demonstration, I'm now seeing all kinds of mossy greenish stuff and obvious signs of decay on the few front teeth that remain in his head.

As I point my new laser into the ear canal, I see scabs and flakes of dead skin resting in what looks to be a dark bed of congealed oils.

Moving down, I'm now, with my fingers, prying apart several of the folds of fat on Harvey's neck, revealing a pasty mixture of sweat and grime.

Harvey has awoken from me pressing on his neck, and I've said to him, "It's okay, it's just me, Waldo," and he's nodded and gone back to sleep.

Now I've plugged my computer into a special photo-microscope device, which I'm holding close to the rim of Harvey's half-closed left eye. On the computer screen I'm now seeing tiny microscopic creatures slurping from the trough of water at the edge of Harvey's eyelids.

As I move the photo microscope through his whiskers and hair, I see more of the same: boulders of dirt, oils, scales, tiny crawling things.

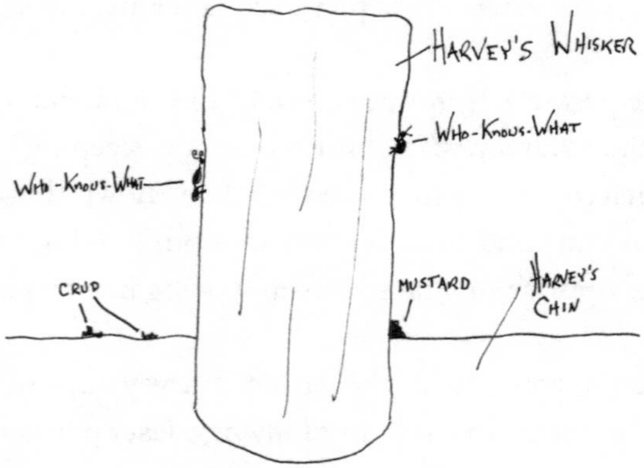

Let's turn now to the Tree beneath which Harvey has passed out. Harvey and the Tree are alike in many ways. For example, once again with the photo microscope, we can see lots of the same kind of crap on the tree that we saw on Harvey—moisture, decay, debris, little scurrying living things.

This is because both Harvey and the tree share Life. Life requires fuel of some type to keep Life going. The getting of fuel and the using of fuel and the getting rid of wastes requires all kinds of fancy tubing. And so both Harvey and the Tree are made up of a dizzying network of systems that sustain the complications of life.

And the time will come when the system fails, and Life must leave them both.

And so, when Harvey and the Tree each say goodbye to Life, what happens next?

Over time, Dead Harvey and Dead Tree, lying side by side at the edge of the park, will both just kind of disappear. Where will they go?

My prediction is, they will both become small bits of Stuff, getting smaller and smaller all the time. And then, moved by wind, moved by water, absorbed by this, gobbled up by that, they shall appear to disappear.

I know you're a detail person, No Pushover, so let's keep going.

You may ask, "How small will the pieces become?"

"Infinitesimally small," I retort. "Until each and every piece is so small that it cannot be cleaved into two."

"Balderdash!" I'm having you bellow. "There is nothing so small that it cannot be made smaller!"

I thank you, No Pushover, for playing into my hands, because now I get to trumpet this in great big capital letters:

YES! YES THERE IS! THERE IS ONE AND ONLY ONE THING THAT CANNOT BE CLEAVED INTO TWO! AND THAT ONE THING IS . . .

GOD!

That's right! God!

You thought God was big? Think again! God's a shrimp! As tiny as things get! The tiniest, eensy-weensiest thing there is!

And when you become that teensy-weensy, YOU CAN BECOME A PART OF ANYTHING THERE IS!

Who knows, No Pushover. Maybe one day in the Forever, you and I will somehow mingle, collide, team up. Wouldn't that be a kick? Looking forward to it.

Your Fan,

Waldo Mellon

Love

Dear Waldo,

The other day I went fishing with my bud Luke and we went to the bait shop and the super-hot bait shop chick told us earthworms were hemafordites if that's even the way you spell it, which she said is what you call something that's both a dude and a chick all in one. And I was thinking to myself, if that's a real thing then I want to be one of them. I fall in love with chicks nonstop everywhere I go. I am one horndog for sure but my love life is not exactly at the level I want it at. And I can't think of anything better than being one of them hemafordites if there is such a thing and skipping the whole dating wahoo altogether and just banging my own self nutty in my basement any time I please. It sure explains the looks of a earthworm. Anyways, Luke said she was just yanking my chain. Was she? Is there such a thing as a hemafordite? I'm just going to sign this as—

Horndog a-lookin for love

Dear Horndog a-lookin for love,

No, the bait-shop girl was not yanking your chain. There is such a thing as a hermaphrodite, and the earthworm is a good example. A single earthworm does indeed have both male and female sex organs.

But Horndog, Sex is one thing. Love is another thing.

A lot of people will tell you a lot of things about what love is and what love isn't, and you will read poems about it and you will hear songs about it and you will not want to eat because of it and you will find nothing that comes close to love in its power to make you cock-eyed with confusion, and love can drive you to rapture and love can drive you to murder.

And yet no one can pinpoint what love is.

This is because love is different for everyone.

But I am happy to tell you what love is not. And if I had a font that blinked on and off in orange neon I would be using it to write this:

Sure, sex turbo-charges love, but sex is no more essential to love than perfect weather is essential to a great vacation.

This to me is what love is: the feeling I get when another living creature convinces me that we are allies in the struggle to be hopeful and kind.

There you have it. I have placed coins into the hands of polite and eager parking attendants, both men and women, for whom I have felt a tingle of love.

So, Horndog, you and the bait girl. I could be wrong, but it sounds to me like it's a good old-fashioned sex thing. Should it come to wild humping, that might be a delight for both of you. But at this point, why not leave Love out of it?

Because here is a common tragedy: as you search for a partner to love and to cherish till death do you part, you will have to put up with the mindless incessant yowling of your ancient reproductive system hell-bent on survival.

The more turned on you are by Beauty, the more deafening and distracting the sex yowl. Because of this racket made by your reproductive wolf pack, you may be tempted to try your luck with that skeleton key to the Sex Palace, that handy shortcut to screwing—the actual blurting of those three words: I . . . Love . . . You.

Beware: It's only much later, when the yowling of the loins subsides, that you will finally hear each other's true music. And when you do, you may find, to your deep sorrow, that it is not a tune you care for, and you will wish you had had a better ear.

Horndog, I say go buy some more bait, and look the bait girl in the eye—really look at her, really take in how she looks back at you—and see what there is to see.

Your Fan,
Waldo Mellon

Chaos

Dear Waldo,

My partner and I have been married thirty-seven years. We still say I love you to each other, but it's a private hunch of mine that sometimes we just say it because it's an easy thing to do and it smooths things out for a while. It feels different than it used to feel. We used to thrill each other. What happened to thrilling each other?

Sincerely,

Thrill Is Gone

Dear Thrill Is Gone,

Have I ever got some fabulous news for you. As you may or may not know, I believe we exist in a chaotic universe and that there's no plan whatsoever. Everything happens not by design but by cold-blooded, heart-breaking randomness. We shape our lives from whatever debris has been swept by chance into our cosmic dustpans, and the trick of making life enjoyable is using our great big brains to separate that debris into shapes that give us the illusion of meaning, which, if you're lucky, can lead to a happy life.

Here's the short version:

Life is making order out of Chaos.

Which brings us, Thrill Is Gone, to my fabulous news: all of life can be divided into three predictable, sequential, manageable, easy-to-understand phases:

1. Q-Time
2. X-Time
3. El-Time

On the grand scale of life, Q-Time is Question Time—Youth. A time for thinking that you don't know very much, that you wish you knew more, and hoping nobody finds out how little you understand about everything.

On the grand scale of life, X-Time is Exclamation Time—Adulthood. A time for thinking that you're really starting to understand things, that you're leaving childhood behind, and that maybe, just maybe, you're better than you think.

On the grand scale of life, El-Time is Ellipsis Time—Old Age. A time for drumming your fingers, for sitting and thinking and waiting. And for accepting.

This same sequence plays out again and again in small ways on a daily basis throughout all of our lives.

We wonder. We discover. We grow tired.

And, Thrill Is Gone, never does it play out with more laughable predictability than in the flophouse you find yourself in at the moment: the Flophouse of Love. You wondered who you would love, you discovered who you would love, and then there arrived those three fucking dots . . .

The good news is that everyone else on the planet has spent time at the El-Time Flophouse. Ask anyone. You'll see. Nobody gets out of town without going there.

Thrill Is Gone, you must have faith. Sooner or later you will slide out of El-Time into Q-Time, and Q-Time will ease into

X-Time, and then—you can count on it—you will be face down in the El-Time Flophouse once again.

And then—HUZZAH! The clouds shall part! The cycle shall repeat itself.

Think about it. Has this not always been so?

And so may I suggest to you an experiment? When someone asks how you're doing, tell the truth in a new way. Say you're Q-Timing. Or say you're X-Timing. Or say you're El-Timing. Wouldn't it be nice if the day comes when everybody just nods and knows exactly what you're talking about?

Be patient. I'm really rooting for you.

Your Fan,

Waldo Mellon

Marriage

Dear Waldo,

Lisa and I are thinking about getting married, but our families are not exactly showcases for success in love. My father's been married four times, my mother's been married three times, my brother's never been married but has three kids by three different mothers. Lisa doesn't know who her real father is, her mother just got divorced for the second time, and her two sisters have five divorces between them and their brother collects restraining orders like they might be worth money someday. But Lisa and I don't just want to get married. We want our marriage to be one of lasting happiness. You got any good ideas about this?

Scared but in love,

Jenny and Lisa

Dear Jenny and Lisa,

As your fragmented, dysfunctional families display so beautifully, marriage can get rough. However, I'm pleased to report that I have developed a simple, four-part survey to determine if you are good candidates for long-term marriage bliss. So please find a comfy place to sit together, Jenny and Lisa, and feel free to consult with each other as you take . . .

Here we go:

1. Imagine that the two of you are sitting on an empty beach, looking out at the sea. Now an incredibly sexy couple strolls by right in front of you.

QUESTION: Which do you guess will happen in the very next moment between the two of you as the beautiful people disappear down the beach?

A. You do not look to each other. You look back at the sea. You say nothing.

B. You turn to each other, release a noise usually made by the Three Stooges.

If either one of you chose A, DO NOT GET MARRIED. I'M NOT JOKING. THE ODDS ARE TOO HIGH IT WILL FAIL. DO. NOT. GET. MARRIED. DO NOT.

Why? Because pretending your beloved's ass is the only ass in the world that makes you hot is a silly lie, and it's a lie that will play out badly.

2. You are strolling down a leafy avenue on a lovely spring day and you hear this screaming argument from inside House A: "I hate your stinking filthy guts!" "I wish we never got married!" "Fuck you!" "Fuck *you*!" "Fuck you times ten!" "Fuck you times twenty!" Continuing on, you pass House B, where another couple sits side by side on the porch, and you hear this being said in controlled, even tones: "I have such contempt for you." "And I for you."

QUESTION: In which house is there a BETTER CHANCE that everything might be fine tomorrow?

(*Helpful Hint: Hate and Contempt are two very different things. You may hate broccoli, but you cannot have contempt for broccoli. You may say you hate Hitler, but what you mean is you have contempt for Hitler.*)

The question, again, is: Is it MORE LIKELY that everything will be fine tomorrow in House A or House B?

If either one of you did not answer House A, FORGET IT. DO NOT GET MARRIED. RUN FOR THE HILLS.

Why? Because hating each other's stinking filthy guts from time to time is a perfectly healthy and acceptable activity in a strong, long-term marriage. Having contempt for your beloved, on the other hand, is not.

3. Imagine that one night your partner has fallen asleep before you. You come to bed and there is your beloved snoring like a rhinoceros. Your partner's eyelids and fingers are twitching, and your partner's lips are flapping and your partner's tongue is lolling on dry lips like a beached whale.

QUESTION: Which of the following choices is CLOSER to what you might be thinking?

A. Holy shit. Look at this thing. It's like roadkill, only now I'm supposed to stop my car, get out, and marry it?

B. Awww.

If your answer is not B, you do not need me to tell you what to do, and fast.

Why? Because when you look down at your sleeping loved one, what you are really seeing is Previews of Coming Attractions. With time, that person you intend to spend the rest of your life with will grow hairs where now there are no hairs, will lose hairs where now there are many hairs, and will get loose in places that were once firm and tight.

By choosing B, you are making a hopeful promise to your loved one that you understand all this, and it will be okay to sit side by side as the two of you enjoy getting all roughed up by time.

4. Have a Farting Contest. Decide between yourselves what the rules will be. But follow through with it. It doesn't matter who wins. The important thing is this: you spend some time farting together.

If both of you did not laugh during this contest, FORGET IT. MOVE ON. SKEDADDLE. NOW.

WHY? I have no idea. I think it may have something to do with my cousin Nanny. But in the years ahead, Jenny and Lisa, when times are hard, when life seems unfunny, you could do worse than to think about that farting contest the two of you held once long ago.

Okay. Survey over. How'd you do? I sure hope this helps.

Your Fan,

Waldo Mellon

Boredom

Dear Waldo,

My mom gets this magazine called *People*, and I try not to look at it but usually I can't help it. Every time I do I feel miserable. The people in *People* are always going places and doing things, and I'm stuck in my boring life at home. We don't have much money because my dad and mom have ordinary boring jobs. What I want to know is, is this the way it's probably going to be with me forever unless I make a fortune somehow? Am I in for a stupid, boring life?

Sincerely,
Wilhelm

Dear Wilhelm,

I have great news for you, young man! You are in for a fabulous life, thanks to an amazing trick I call the Magic Watering Can/ Magic Shriveled-Up Sponge Trick.

I know what you're thinking. You're thinking, "Boy, that's a bad name for a trick." I agree. Nonetheless, like it or not, that's what I've named it.

And Wilhelm, it's a trick that will change your life for the better on a regular basis after you get over its name.

Here's how this mind-blowing trick is performed:

First, choose something—anything—to focus on. Whatever

you have chosen now becomes your Magic Shriveled-Up Sponge. Anything in the Universe, including the Universe itself, can be your Magic Shriveled-Up Sponge.

Once you've chosen your Magic Shriveled-Up Sponge, it's time to wheel in the Magic Watering Can. The reason you have to wheel it in is because it's huge. In fact, it's infinitely huge. This Magic Watering Can of yours never, ever runs out of water. But there's a problem. A can as big as that is difficult to tip, and unless the water pours from the spout, you cannot perform the critical phase of the trick, which is pouring the Magic Water onto your Magic Shriveled-Up Sponge.

Here's where the trick gets a little tricky:

ONE THING AND ONE THING ONLY CAN CAUSE YOUR MAGIC WATERING CAN TO TIP:

Curiosity

As I write this, I notice an ant climbing across the sill of my window. Ordinarily I'd either ignore it or just blow it away. But this time I'm going to make it my Magic Shriveled-Up Sponge.

Hmmm. Where are its eyes?

Does it have a heart? No, I think I've been told that bugs don't have hearts.

Then how does this little guy distribute the food it eats to the rest of its body?

And look at the parts of its body and the things that connect the parts.

And where's it going?

I'm gonna touch it with my pencil. Look at it go! Does it feel panic?

And with each question, with each new splash of Curiosity, I spill my Magic Water on my Magic Shriveled-Up Sponge, and look what happens:

THE SPONGE CHANGES SHAPE!
IT BECOMES MORE!

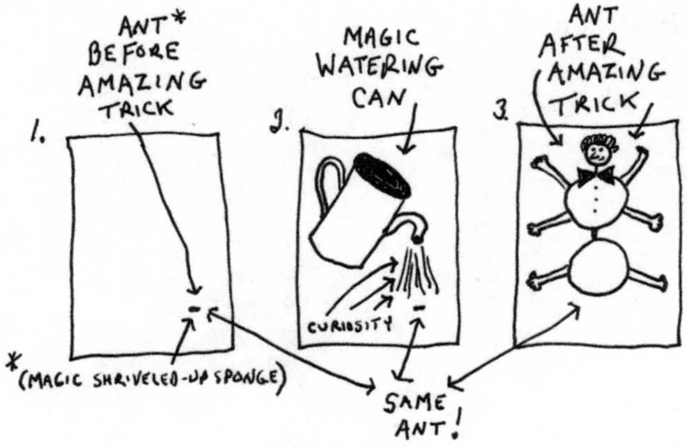

I now have a relationship with the little guy. It's made me wonder. As I consider it more closely, its front legs have become arms and the little thingies on the ends of its arms have become hands. The little round head is kind of, well, cute. I've begun to glimpse ANOTHER FULL LIFE.

What if I do the same thing to, say, the Civil War?

Or to the details of an archway?

Or to the beauty of a ball bearing?

Or to a leaf?

Or to my fingernails?

Or to two sides of an argument you thought had only one side?

My god, the Heartbreak! The Strength!

Do you see what this means, Wilhelm? When you say you're bored, all you're really saying is that you can't find the energy at this particular moment to be curious. The solution? It's already in you. Get off your butt! Splash around in the universe! Now off with you! Go!

Your Fan,

Waldo Mellon

Loveliness

Dear Waldo,

It's 4 a.m. and I must admit to you that I am in a terrible way. I cannot sleep, and this is not like me. I'm sixty-seven, and my husband is seven years older than I am, and when we go to bed at night and I hold him I can feel the loosening of his skin, and on the back of his neck are little things he's never had before, and the thought of not having him anymore is too much for me. We have three wonderful children who are grown and out in the world now, and the idea of the phone ringing and then one of them never coming home again is so awful it seems to break into little pieces as I think this. And I'll hear my pulse in my ears, and then I'll think that my heart is just this moving thing inside of me that I have nothing to do with really, and outside it's so dark, and I just want to curl up with my babies and my beloved and say it's okay, it's okay, it's okay. And I can see my reflection in the window now. An old lady sitting in front of the fire, writing and crying, writing and crying, except it's not a real fire, the gas and the logs are fake, but here's the honest truth: I put my tongue to the corner of my mouth and my tears seem so delicious and the crazy thing is I am loving this moment, just loving it.

After I wrote the last sentence a while has gone by in which I cried so deeply I began to worry about my back, but now I feel so sleepy. Isn't that something? How I can feel sleepy with all this in my head? Well, maybe I'll send this letter tomorrow and maybe I won't. If I do, it does not require a response.

Sincerely,
Helen Sammers

Dear Helen,

I'm delighted you decided to send your letter because it gives me an opportunity to focus on a concept of "Getting It." "Getting It" is most commonly linked with jokes, and so I'm going to tell you one right now:

A married couple lives by the beach and they're throwing a party, and the wife asks her husband to go collect some sea snails so she can make escargot. So the guy goes down to the water and begins collecting snails into a pail when he meets an absolutely beautiful woman sunbathing. They talk for a while and then she invites him into her beachside cabana. They have a few drinks and before you know it they're making love. And then the guy falls asleep. Three hours later he wakes up to the horror of his situation. He throws on his clothes, grabs the pail of snails, dashes back to his house. And as he leaps up the steps to his door he trips, dumping the pail of snails onto the walkway. Now the door opens and it's his wife scowling down at him. A horrible pause. The guy turns to the snails on the ground. "C'mon, guys, you're doing great, almost there, keep it up, doing good, almost there . . ."

"Getting it" happens instantaneously, like at the punchline of a joke. It does not involve the slow plodding of understanding. It's as if the tips of two live-wires touch—one connected to you and the other connected to everything else—and suddenly a flash of order leaps from the chaos and is gone as soon as you glimpse it.

The kind of "getting it" I'm talking about now is much bigger, much more powerful, much more special, than the getting of a joke. You at 4 a.m., in the glow of fake logs burning in a gas fire, weeping at you have no firm idea what. That, too, is "getting it."

A sudden flash of fragility and beauty and desperation and sweetness and panic and magnificence and helplessness and gratitude, and then it's gone.

Moment over.

No understanding.

Never to happen exactly like that again.

I say lucky you.

Your Fan,

Waldo Mellon

Fighting

Dear Waldo,

I would just like to point out that there's another kind of "getting it," such as when I was a kid and my old man said "Now you're really going to get it." Or more recently, my wife and me had a fight you wouldn't believe and Corinna threw a new toaster oven and a chair at me. I look back at what I said and the way I was and I go "What the hell is wrong with me?" It was like I was somebody else. Corinna just came in and read what I got so far and said to add it was scary. She's right. Our fight was scary. Is there something we can do so it doesn't happen again?

Bing and Corinna

Dear Bing and Corinna,

I think I have some very good news for you. What the two of you took was a trip everybody takes from time to time. You took a trip to the Blowzone.

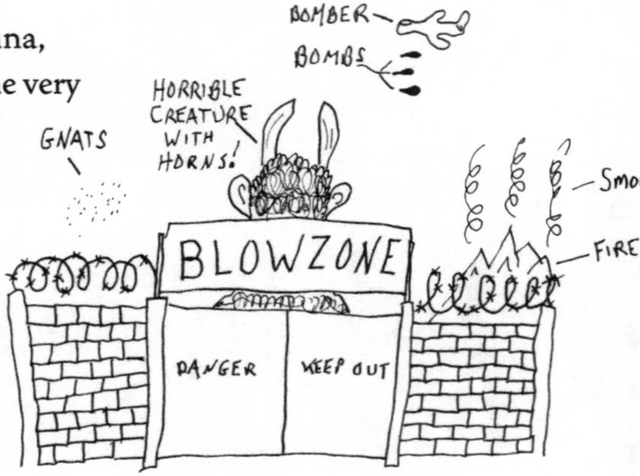

It's a horrible place, the Blowzone. Just horrible.

How can you tell if you have, indeed, entered the Blowzone? The signs are clear and obvious:

1. You're having an argument.

2. You feel you're losing. You reach into your Communication Tool Box for another tool—uh-oh. Empty.

3. What You're Saying becomes What You're Yelling.

4. What You're Yelling becomes a very distant relative of What You Were Saying.

5. You switch your primary goal from Trying to Say What You Think Is True, to Trying to Say What You Think Will Hurt.

6. With your own ears, you hear yourself becoming a child. An unpleasant child.

7. Things that aren't meant to be thrown begin to seem delightfully throwable.

8. A few of your cells, somewhere dark, find this event exhilarating, almost amusing, but the rest of your cells do not.

Sound familiar, Bing and Corinna?

Welcome to the Blowzone.

It's a dangerous place. Horrible things happen there. Ducking toaster ovens, for example.

Why do we behave this way? If you ask me, it's because evolution has made our advanced intelligence our ace in the hole. The skunk gets That Smell. The giraffe gets That Neck. The porcupine gets Those Quills. Us, we get a less reliable problem solver: the Ability to Reason.

And when our ace in the hole fails, when our words fail us, we're goners.

Bing and Corinna, there is only one law of the land inside the Blowzone, and it is as constant as physics:

The longer you stay there, the worse things will get.

You must get out of the Blowzone.

Here's how it's done:

1. You say, either out loud or to yourself, "Uh-oh, I'm in the Blowzone."

2. You turn on your heels, move your body away from anyone else in the Blowzone, the farther away the better. If you're being followed, pick up speed.

3. Sit somewhere. Relax. Wait for the lunatic we're all capable of being to climb out of you and to stagger away. You may wave bye-bye if you want.

4. When you're ready, consider the wording of an apology for the part you played in the horrors of your trip to the Blowzone.

5. Rise, deliver the apology.

And for crying out loud, practice. Practice, practice, practice.

Your Fan,

Waldo Mellon

Decisions

Dear Waldo,

I got a problem. When I go out to dinner, no matter who I'm with, I order and the second the waiter leaves I wish I had ordered something else. When I go on a trip, I wonder if I would be having more fun if I were someplace else. Even when I'm buying, say, peas, I stand there forever looking over the pea selection. My friends say I can't make a decision about anything. Is there anything I can do about this?

Signed,
Smegma

Dear Smegma,

Really? Smegma? Are you sure about your name being Smegma? Okay. Smegma, I'm delighted to say that there is plenty you can do about your problem. No matter how many decisions you're faced with, you are really only making one decision again and again and again:

YES OR NO.

When life seems easy, that's because for a lovely, delicate stretch of time the Yesses are clear Yesses and the Nos are clear Nos. What ruins the fun is the onset of a horrible condition called Maybe.

Maybe happens when a brain develops the ability to formulate the notion of options. Those lucky amoebic idiots, for example, know no Maybe. For them, and we can only guess for how many other living things, there is only the easy bliss of Yes or No.

Our brains, however, are the greatest question-formulating machines on the planet, which makes us, sadly . . .

And that, Smegma, is your problem. You're stuck in Maybe-time. Maybe-time is no damn fun. During Maybe-time, passionate commitment to anything is impossible. It is a shapeless, doughy time in which you wonder about eating too many sweets, and the hours hemorrhage into oblivion, only to return later to taunt you with that sinking feeling that life is passing you by.

But I have an easy, ground-breaking exercise you can do to get rid of Maybe-time forever. You see, Smegma, the sensation of Yes is as different from the sensation of No as the sensation of Lust is different from the sensation of Love. That is, the sensations your body feels in each instance are very different. And so what I'm going to do, Smegma, is I'm going to give you a series of ten specially formulated questions to which I want you to answer either Yes or No.

However, I do not what you to answer them out loud. Instead, I just want you to focus on the feeling inside your body when you think "Yes," and the feeling inside your body when you think "No."

Remember: only Yes or No . . .

Okay. Let's begin.

1. Would you like to be held by someone you love?

2. Would you like some chips of glass to be pressed into your eyeballs?

3. Do you want the sun to explode, terminating life on earth in a sudden scalding fireball?

4. Would you like an all-expenses-paid vacation to a holiday spot of your choosing?

5. Do you want to sit down hard on a giant red-hot spinning screw?

6. Do you want good health?

7. Do you want me to knock your front teeth out with a short-handled hammer?

8. Do you like being dry and warm and comfortable?

9. Do you like kind and honest people?

10. Do you like being crushed by an anvil inside a safe?

These questions have been scientifically prepared by me in my lab so that your responses should be unsullied by even the slightest hint of indecision.

This, of course, is not the Real World. When questions are generated by the Real World, your yesses and nos will appear blurred through the fog of cultural expectations. And therefore it becomes critical, Smegma, that you become skilled in recognizing the difference in feeling between Yes and No.

Here's a good rule of thumb:

YOUR HEART KNOWS; YOUR BRAIN GUESSES.

The better you get at recognizing difference in the feeling of Yes and No, the less you will be hounded by Maybe. But know this: Maybe will never completely go away. Here's what must be done with it:

TREAT MAYBE AS NO.

Any time you're about to do something important, DO NOT DO IT if you feel unsure. DO NOT DO IT until you can get that feeling, that lovely feeling, however fleeting, of a firm YES.

Be patient.

Whenever in doubt, take your specially formulated ten-question exercise out of your wallet, and practice practice practice.

Focus on the feeling. Wait for the feeling of a firm Yes. Wait for the feeling of a firm No.

I hope this helps.

Your Fan,

Waldo Mellon

Aging

Dear Waldo,

I'm eighty-one. My wife has died and we had no children. I live in the city and I wandered into a little place where I didn't know it would be all young people, but it was. I had a book that I'm enjoying very much, and I sat there reading and having one of their soups. A young girl came in and sat down nearby. Through no fault of her own, I was made to be miserable. All my life I have been made miserable by attractive women, but particularly by any woman who does one of two things, or two of two things. The things are, having long hair that sometimes falls over one eye and then gets swished back either by her hand or by the quick lovely movement of her head; or wearing an article of clothing that has such a big neck hole that one of her shoulders pops out in a yummy way. This girl I'm writing to you about had both.

I put my soup spoon down and had to just go home. I am sitting here now in my apartment eating cream of wheat mixed with half and half and seeing that hair, that shoulder, and a worrisome thing is happening: I think I'm becoming a creep. I'm not finding anything to care about tomorrow. I've lived a long time. Maybe I should call it quits. What do you think?

Sincerely,

Oscar

Dear Oscar,

No, I definitely don't think you should call it quits. You're sufficiently healthy to read. You're sufficiently healthy to walk. Your appetite seems good. And you appear to be a burden to no one. Just being a Thing That Has Life In It is so unlikely that you'd be nuts not to keep it going as long as you can just to see what happens next.

The great news is that your complaint, as I hear it, is not about health. No, your complaint is a much jollier one: that, to use a version of your word, your Days Of Yumminess are behind you.

Turn-ons are goofy. But goofy or not, being turned on is a kick, and Oscar, I say enjoy it.

Go back to that place where you had soup, but go without a book. Just sit and watch as if observing from the stands an elegant and thrilling game you used to play.

And if all goes well, and if you're lucky, you will not have to wait long for your face to register a smile you don't even realize you're making, a smile of poignant and selfless and deep enjoyment.

Your Fan,

Waldo Mellon

Good and Bad

Dear Waldo,

My husband and I have had a running argument throughout our lives together about a particular issue. We both have embarrassingly high-paying jobs, and so we've made a rather substantial bet with each other about who is right and who is wrong. We've polled many of our friends, but the results have been inconclusive, and so we've agreed to consult you as the final arbiter. Whatever you say goes. The issue is this: I contend that people are basically good. My husband contends that people are basically bad. Who wins?

With Fingers Crossed,
Emma Dingman

Dear Emma,

My brother and I have a close childhood friend who, after more than four years, is finally climbing out of the deep dark hole made by a heartbreaking divorce. Our friend is a big, sweet, furry fellow, and you have to make room for his laugh, and to emphasize a point he might bang his meaty fist on the table. But when he talks about mistakes he's made, or his kids, it's a soft and different thing.

Last week, clueless about dating after twenty-four years of marriage, he came by my brother's house so that we could help him get ready for a blind date my brother had arranged for him.

Our friend, who is a very good athlete, told us that when he used to get ready for a big game in high school, he got the same feeling in his stomach that he was getting now about this blind date.

Then he went back out to his car, returned with a change of clothes on a hanger, and he disappeared into the bathroom to take a shower.

Through the bathroom door, my brother and his wife and my wife and I called loudly to our friend as he showered. We discussed with him the benefits of shampoo and conditioner. We discussed deodorants.

And then the four of us went from the bathroom door back to the kitchen to wait for our friend to present himself.

Soon he arrived at the kitchen table. He had combed his wet hair, and he was in his new clothes, and this fifty-five year old man, father of four, stood before us like a hopeful schoolboy.

He let us walk around him and around him. He let us sniff him. He let us make small adjustments to his hair. He let us straighten his collar. When we wondered about his sweater, he took it off, and once again we walked around him and around him, picking at this, adjusting that.

And then he put on his reading glasses to examine the little map we had drawn for him to find the house in which his blind date lived.

And then our childhood friend walked out the door and off he went, with all of us waving good luck from the driveway.

My brother and his wife and my wife and I returned to the kitchen table and sat, happy and sad, as if our son had just left for the prom.

On the drive home my wife and I listened to a story on the radio about child prostitution in America. Children were being bought and sold for the purposes of sex, and not just a few. Thousands and thousands. A thirteen-year-old told her story, which began when she was four. Highway rest stops, the story reported, were a popular site for the exchange of children and money.

And so, Emma, I'm sorry that I will be of no use in settling your bet with your husband. Because the answer to your question depends entirely upon where you choose to look, and how you interpret what you see.

Here's the best idea I can come up with: choose to look somewhere bad, and then send the wager money in a direction that might make bad less bad.

Your Fan,

Waldo Mellon

Crying

Dear Waldo,

I find myself blubbering an awful lot. For example, me and my best friend went hunting last week, and I got nothing and he got a doe. I'm about twice as big as he is, so after we gutted the deer, I was carrying it out, and we were just walking along when I made the mistake of telling him about what happened yesterday. What happened yesterday was that I drove my daughter to the airport so she could fly off to college, and I walked back to the parking lot, and then I just sat there in my truck for a while blubbering away because off she went for who knows how long.

My friend couldn't believe his ears. He smacked me on the back of the head and called me a pussy and I said "Oh yeah?" and dropped the deer and stomped away. Later he came over to my place and we just sat around for a while. Then he went back out and came back in with deer steaks all wrapped up and he said "Here." And he just left. Looking at that meat, the truth is I felt like blubbering again but did not. My problem is, I believe I blubber more than most. Is it something I should do something about?

Yours Truly,

C.

Dear C.,

When you cried at the airport, your fuses were not blown by

danger, but by the raining down of fragmented thoughts. By the ganging up of quieter forces, such as the thought of never seeing your little girl again. By your own aging. By the off-stage rustling of distant blunders, shapeless regrets, vague detached panic. This kind of quiet emotional bombardment is common at milestone events such as weddings and funerals, and it's not far from childhood panic in its confusion.

The bigger question is how come your pal smacked you on the back of the head.

He saw crying as a sign of weakness.

Which leads us to the sexual implications of crying. On a superficial level, crying and sex have this in common: when you do either one, you're apt to make an unbecoming face, and then out come fluids.

But more significantly, if a man allows himself to do what women do, which is to cry when they feel like crying—uh-oh. Now a man's Man-ness comes into question.

Not good for King of the Jungle.

Now he might have to shine some light into that darkness beneath the deep layers of pink-ruffled horror where the sleeping homosexual in every male on the planet waits to be shaken awake.

Therefore, I don't think your pal is about to cry any time soon, C., and he'll probably keep swatting you every time you do. But don't let that stop you. Whenever you got a real beauty of a lump going in your throat, I say blubber away. In my experience, a good cry never fails to improve things.

And I'm going to make a prediction: Public Bawling is going to be the next big thing. Someone of high international repute is going to cry openly on television about the state of the world and then justify it with clarity and eloquence.

Finally, C., I'm guessing you might be able to get a good cry going thinking about that buddy of yours who's all locked up in this regard.

Your Fan,

Waldo Mellon

Opinions

Dear Waldo,

I'm fifteen, almost sixteen, and lots of times I lie in bed at night worrying about what people think of me. Such as I went to a new camp last summer and we were all sitting around the campfire telling stories about the scariest thing that ever happened to us. And then it was my turn but I couldn't think of a single story because the smoke from the fire was blowing right at me and I even got up and moved, but wherever I went the stupid smoke kept blowing in my face and my eyes kept burning. I tried to say something but I choked on the smoke and everybody kept looking at me and it was horrible. I guess my question is, is there any way to make people think about me the way I want them to?

Sincerely,
Andrew Flilsh

Dear A.,

The bad news, I'm sorry to say, is that my answer is no. There is absolutely no way to make people think what you want them to think about you.

But here's a fact: their Opinion of you is no more real than the dreams of the Easter Bunny in your dream of the Easter Bunny dreaming.

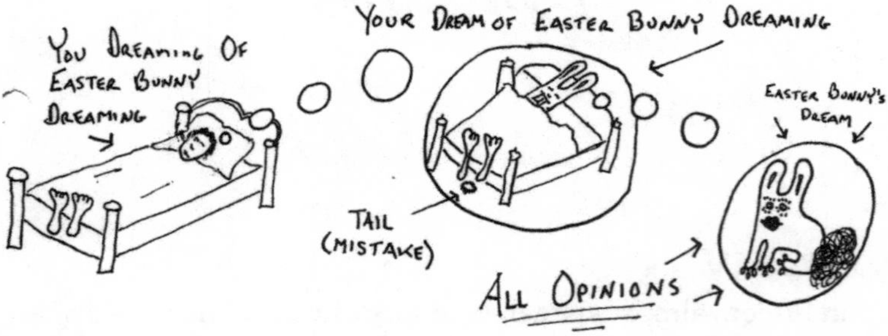

And so, lying in bed worrying about Other People's Opinions of You is exactly like lying in bed worrying about the direction of that stupid wind blowing smoke in your eyes. You can try this and you can try that, but it's not in your control.

However, the good news is that there is something you can do. Because every Opinion of you that anybody has ever had can be separated into two piles:

1. Opinions of You That You Hear About
2. Opinions of You That You DON'T Hear About

Of those two piles, Andrew, the bigger pile by far, and I do mean by far, is pile #2: Opinions of You That You DON'T Hear About.

Most people don't tell other people directly what they think about them unless it's something nice.

And this means that most of what people think about you—Opinions of You That You DON'T Hear About—can be stuffed into one gigantic sack and tossed out. Because there is nothing you can do about them.

Heave-ho. Good riddance.

However, the other tiny sack—the little itty-bitty sack of Opinions of You That You DO Hear About—what you have there, Andrew, is something quite different. What you have there is

A BAG OF GOLD!

Because now you've really got something valuable to work with. Now you get a rare glimpse into what is inside someone else's head concerning You. If the Opinion That You DO Hear About is good, terrific. Throw yourself a little party in your head.

But if you find out that somebody has said something bad about you, something that makes you upset in some way, pay special attention. Because your response may be a sign that there is some Truth to it. Look at it as a gift. Thanks to the Opinion of this person, you have an opportunity to get to the bottom of the matter. In a perfect world, you would go to that person and you would have a nice discussion to find out if what you heard was true. The main goal would not be to change that person's mind but to find out why that person thinks the way that person thinks.

And so, Andrew, here's what it boils down to: If people think you're more wonderful than you think you are, maybe they see things in you that you don't see. If people think you're less wonderful than you think you are, maybe they're seeing things in you that you don't see.

Check it all out. Why not?

And if you start to really worry about all these things that are out of your control, remember that camp fire, and that stupid wind.

Your Fan,

Waldo Mellon

Blues

Hey Waldo My Main Man!

Loved, just loved, your letter on crybabies. You rule. You and me are exactly the same! Because we both just want everybody to cheer up!! What's the big problem??? Just be happy, that's our motto, right, big guy!!! I told someone yesterday I was happy as a lark and he picked me up and tossed me into a broom closet! What's with that?!?!?! My question is, how come when some people aren't happy they can't just snap out of it and try to brighten this dreary ol' world up, like you and me with our positive attitudes and our upbeat comments and our cool way of striding around? C'mon, sad sacks! Cheer up like me 'n Waldo! What's the probbo, slobbo?!?

In Love with Life!

Paul Lee Anna

(Not my real name, but do you get it? Ha ha ha!!)

Dear Paul Lee Anna,

While I nearly chewed a hole in my cheek as I read your letter, I will nonetheless try to respond to your question by focusing upon what feels at the moment like fresh air: unhappiness.

I'm not talking about good old-fashioned sorrow, which is a clear and healthy and immediate response to an event you can put your finger on, such as the loss of a loved one or the end of anything lovely.

And I'm also not talking about that fly-by-night form of unhappiness that loop-di-loops in and out upon the whimsy of mood.

No, the unhappiness I'm talking about is the industrial-strength brand, the vague and shapeless kind, rooted in nothing and everything, the kind that just settles on you like a mist and enters your pores and your lungs and your hair.

And I'm pleased to announce that I have devised an instrument with which to measure how Happy or Unhappy you are. It's called…

THE BLUES-O-METER

The great news is that the Blues-O-Meter doesn't cost anything and all you need is two hands.

Here's how it works: Your level of contentment is a measure of the distance between what you think you want and what you think you have. That distance can be measured by your hands. By spreading your hands as far apart as possible, you would be expressing the maximum distance between what you think you want and what you think you have. That is, you would be indicating that you believe you have none of the things you want. This would be uncommon.

By bringing your palms together in front of your chest, as in prayer, you would be indicating that you believe you have everything you want. This too would be uncommon.

Most people place their hands somewhere in the middle.

And now I'm going to tell

you about a friend I once had. He was handsome and smart and funny, and he played guitar and sang and he loved tennis and Pink Floyd, and his parents loved him and his sisters loved him and I loved him and everyone who really knew him loved him. One day this wonderful guy tore a single sheet of lined notepaper into three smaller pieces, and upon each of those scraps he wrote a few words and then, after he put each short note into an addressed stamped envelope and dropped it into a mailbox, he went into the woods and he put the barrel of a gun into his mouth and later someone who did not know him found him at around the same time his parents and his girlfriend and I were reading his goodbye notes to us.

I'm sure that if I had asked him, there in the woods, to measure his Unhappiness on his Blues-O-Meter, he would have put the gun down and stretched his arms out as wide as they could possibly go. At the very least what he wanted was a little Hope, but apparently there was none to be found.

If I had been with him in the woods I might have said: See? This Unhappiness of yours, which seems so vast, can be no bigger than you, no greater than the reach of your outstretched arms? And look how small you are, how tiny beneath these trees, beneath the huge sky.

Exactly, I imagine him saying to me, relaxing his arms and then reaching for his gun. Exactly.

And this is all I'd be left with: Wait. Please wait. Please. Name one thing that never changes. One thing. One thing. Because nothing lasts forever. Nothing stays the same. This too shall pass. This too shall pass. You will want to go to the movies again. You will fall into a book again. You will want to get lost in a restaurant menu again. You will be choosy about toothpaste again. You will buy something in a store just to get change for the parking meter again. You will be fed up with me again. You will. You will. You will. Just wait. Just please wait. Just please wait. Please. Just please wait . . .

What I'm saying to you, Paul Lee Anna, is that sometimes unhappiness has less to do with choices made than with the mysteries of chemistry. Sometimes your will is powerless. Sometimes all you can do to tell the truth is say nothing and then spread your hands as far apart as they will go.

Waldo Mellon

War

Dear Waldo,

You're going to think I'm being a smart aleck but I'm not. I really want to know: How come there's so many wars all the time? No other animals I know of have wars. How come we do?

Yours Truly,

Big Chicken

Dear Big Chicken,

You ask a very important question, and a tough one, and I'll do my best to answer it but in a roundabout way.

The other day I read a flyer stapled to a telephone pole. It said this:

Looking for housemate. Do you enjoy sharing delicious, home-cooked organic vegetarian meals, gardening, sitting on the front porch watching the seasons change, playing music, making art, and spending time with people you live with? Would you be excited to have occasional community gatherings such as potluck dinners and skill-sharing workshops right in your own home? If so, maybe you'd enjoy living in our fun, supportive, energy-efficient cooperative living space.

Big Chicken, when I tell you that as I read that flyer a loathing rose within me like stagnant steam from a sidewalk subway grate, it is not meant to be a commentary on community housing. No, it is an uneasy confession for something that I cannot explain.

And it's no comfort to know that I'm not alone in this kind of small-minded looniness. Why does my brother get a rash on his neck around Morris dancers? How come my best friend crosses the street to avoid a mime? What's with despising Neil Diamond?

There's no rational explanation, because we are not rational creatures. We are works in progress, capable of having serious, ugly feelings about people who enjoy Big Macs, about people who have private jets, about people who pierce their tongues. Doesn't it take just a few more leaps in lunacy before larger groups of humans, beefed up by a steady diet of misinformation and all jazzed up on paranoia, begin hating them other races, hating them other countries, hating them other ways of going about life?

Say, I got an idea! Let's have a war!

At the same time, we're wise enough to have come up with a simple rule, which, if followed faithfully, would eliminate war completely:

DO UNTO OTHERS
AS YOU WOULD HAVE OTHERS
DO UNTO YOU

Now there's a slogan! It's so astoundingly simple. Do you want someone sticking a bayonet between your ribs? Me either. Then don't stick one between someone else's ribs.

Ya wanna be bombed? Me either! Then don't go a-bombing.

Ya wanna be lied to or cheated on or stolen from? Who does?

What's the big problem here? Why are we so incapable of obeying such a simple suggestion?

Here's why: Because we are not rational creatures in control of our actions. We think we are, which is proof that we are not.

And so, in conclusion, Big Chicken, I guess my best, most honest answer to your great question about why there are so many wars is this:

Dunno. Just dunno.

My best guess: our fabulous species still got us some flaws.

Your Fan,

Waldo Mellon

Me Me Me

Dear Waldo,

What makes you think you're such a big shot, telling everybody this and that like you're some great big know-it-all even though you got no special training or credentials or anything to make yourself more credible? Also, do you have T-shirts with Waldo Mellon on them? Or hats?

Pissed Off, but Would Like a Hat,

Cammy

Dear Cammy,

Thank you for your note. You are absolutely right. I have no special credentials or training. And I know that right after hollering fire, the best way to clear a crowded room is to yell "Anybody wanna hear my philosophy of life?"

So why am I doing this?

To answer this question, let me tell you about something that happened yesterday. I was standing in a line at the bank, and as the line turned sharply I found myself facing, less than a foot away, an elderly woman—she must've been eighty—and we exchanged brief oh-boy-stuck-in-line-again smiles.

The line was moving very slowly, and so I spent a good three minutes in the unnatural circumstance of being face to face with an old person I was not talking to. In this configuration I was able to look at her—I mean really look at her—and I could see now that her eyebrows were really just penciled-on drawings of eyebrows, and that the flush of her cheeks was really crimson powder caught in the pores, and that her lipstick bled like tiny insect legs into the creases around her mouth.

Someone sneezed, and my attention turned to the security guard blowing his nose. He was a nice-looking gentleman, maybe seventy, with a magnificent silver-gray pompadour that rose like a surfer's wave a good three inches above the beach of his forehead. He folded his handkerchief just so, and tucked it back into the breast pocket of his security-guard blazer, flaring the exposed edge before looking up.

Cammy, when it comes right down to it, we are all just animals that want to be special in some way. We want to be looked up to. We want to look as good as we possibly can.

And so, in answer to your question, I would have to say that these words you are reading are my drawn-on eyebrows, my pompadour, my lipstick-red lips, my way of hoping to be special.

Your Fan,

Waldo Mellon

P.S. As far as hats and T-shirts go, I have no plans in this area. If that changes, you will be the first to know.

Your Chickens

Dear Waldo,

I've known Carla ever since we were little girls in kindergarten. We were best friends right up through high school. But now we're forty-six, and when she calls, I don't pick up the phone. Our politics are completely different. She never asks me about me. She has lots of things to say about everything, and mostly she's angry and sarcastic. Then at the end she always tells me how much she loves me and I feel bad, hearing her voice and remembering the way it was when we were little. Why can't I pick up the phone and talk to this person I once loved?

Sincerely,
Jane

Dear Jane,

A while ago a neighbor called to tell me she'd found a chicken in her barn and had no idea how it got there. She knew we had a few chickens, so she wondered if we might want this one. My wife said sure. So that evening we drove down the hill, cornered the horrified chicken, and brought it home.

The next morning we discovered that this new chicken had a big gooey hole beneath one wing, an ugly wound no one had noticed until now.

Let's back up to the phone call. If our neighbor had called and said "Hello, I got a chicken in my barn with a big gooey festering hole in its side and would you like to add it to your flock," we would have sputtered out some polite version of "What, are you fucking kidding?"

What we said instead was "Absolutely!" And when we said that, the chicken with the gooey hole became ours. That is, our "yes" transformed the chicken from Big Flapping Thing with Concealed Oozing Gooey Wound to Feathered Creature Sleeping Feet Up in Lap of Wife.

We named the chicken Moxie. Moxie is thriving. All because we said some form of this word: "okay."

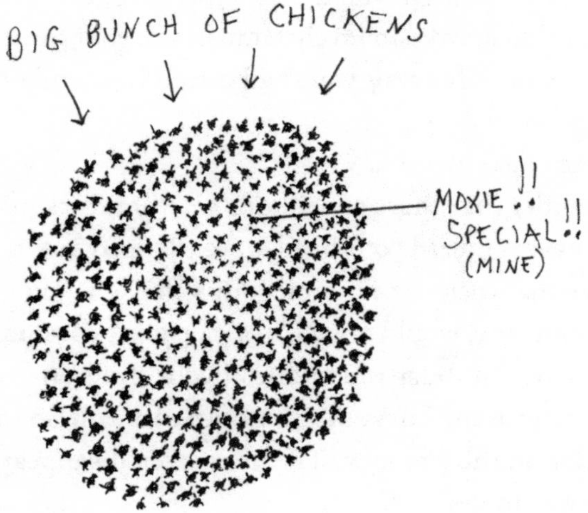

There is no question about it: what you consider to be yours makes all the difference. You pick out two small earrings from all the billions of earrings there are on the planet—Presto! They take on the magic of your choosing. Same with a dress. Or a car. Or a parakeet.

Or a person.

And so, Jane, here's what I'm asking you to do. Find a comfy place where you will not be pestered. And think about those chickens in your life that won your attention, that smacked you sweetly in a certain way. That surprised you with kindness. That made you think slightly differently...

Chickens you fell in love with...

Chickens that made you feel shy...

Chickens that startled you with the threat of new possibilities...

Chickens you don't see anymore but can't forget...

Chickens that broke your heart...

Chickens that brought you to rages you are grateful for...

Chickens that starred in lovely fantasies in your head...

Chickens whose funerals you shall certainly attend no matter what...

Those are your chickens.

And consider this: there are billions of other chickens out there that never entered your head, never flapped out in front of you. Realize that these are all somebody's chickens too.

Just as you, Jane, would howl at the sky if one of your chickens—say, your husband or one of your children—was disappearing into the forest in the mouth of a wolf, so too would everyone else on the planet wail if the chicken disappearing into the woods was theirs.

So here's a suggestion: The next time your childhood friend Carla calls, pick up. It's perfectly fine to hold the phone away from your ear while this chicken of yours blathers on and on. This will have nothing to do with your appreciation for Carla, or with your gratitude for her being in your life. To be picked out as a special chicken, as you have been by Carla, is an honor. So what if she has a gooey hole or two? Who doesn't? I sure do. And before you hang up, you might want to tell Carla you love her too. Because the fact is, when you really get down to it, you do. She's one of your chickens.

Your Fan,
Waldo Mellon

Combos

Dear Waldo,

I'm a security guard at a federal prison, and I have a question about these chickens of yours. I got a good-sized flock all locked up. When you say that life is hard, and that it's all chaos, no offense but I get the feeling that you have not seen hard living or real chaos. Come to work with me someday and I will show you what I am talking about. My question to you is, what should we do with these caged humans of mine? I mean this: if some of them could grab me they would bite into me, tear away chunks of me, and then spit those chunks onto my boots. They like my boots because they are expensive boots and so they want them, and because they cannot have them they resent them and they resent me and therefore they would enjoy spitting chunks of my flesh onto them. These caged animals are my chickens. Is there nothing to be done with these animals other than to keep them in cages?

Jerome

Dear Jerome,

I know under the circumstances it's in bad taste to do what I'm doing at the moment, which is dancing in a tight circle and screaming "Yes!" at the ceiling. Because thanks to your letter, I now have the opportunity to share with you my Combo Theory.

Jerome, remember when you were in high school and you had a locker? And that locker would not open unless you twisted the little knob this way and that way in exactly the right sequence? That sequence of numbers was your Combo.

Well, Jerome, school is not the only thing with lockers and Combos. People have them too. Everybody on the planet is a locker room full of lockers.

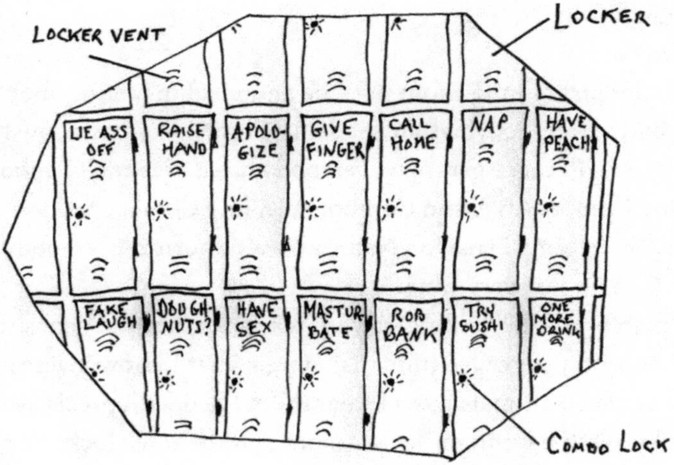

Some of our lockers have real simple Combos that we are fully aware of, and some have Combos that are so impossibly complicated that we haven't a clue.

Take, for example, the Get Married Locker. That particular locker of mine didn't spring open until I was forty-one. I lucked out. My wife and I agree that we are pleasantly stunned by our daily contentment. We have become helplessly devoted to the wild swings of life together and to the friends and family swinging with us.

Yet I am convinced that in both of our locker rooms, each of us has an Infidelity Locker.

That is, there exists some sequence of events—no matter how mind-bogglingly against the odds—that would set tumblers in motion in precisely the required sequence and then a door springs open and the dark of a never-before-opened locker spills out and...

Huh??

You did what??

With who??

I'm not just talking about my wife and me. I'm talking about everybody. Everybody has an Infidelity Combo. And that's just for starters. Because get this: Everybody has a Stealing Combo. A Lying Combo. An Arson Combo. A Killing Combo. Name a crime. Name a misbehavior. Name an act of horror. Everybody has a Combo for everything.

Which brings us, Jerome, to your terrific question: What's to be done with your caged humans? Here's what I know: Every one of those caged animals has a locker room filled with precisely the same lockers I have in my locker room and the same lockers you have in your locker room. Lockers of enlightenment. Lockers of redemption. Lockers of rebirth.

The Combo sequence might begin with a dream, or with a single line in a book, or with an unexpected act of kindness, or with anything that presents a distant light.

Such as you turning a little knob that begins the sequence of the Combo to your locker of Forgiveness.

Your Fan,

Waldo Mellon

Life

Dear Waldo,

My moron brother Lance is obsessed with the idea that there's millions and millions of other planets with life on them. How do I break the news to him that he's just plain nuts?

Sincerely,

Bruno

Dear Bruno,

Before I answer your question, I'd like to point out that there is no such thing as a moron or an idiot or an imbecile. There are only living things that know different things from what you know.

To answer your question, let's take a look at this thing called Life that your brother is talking about. Life is a fabulous against-all-odds Chemical Stunt. Some Stuff mixes with some other Stuff and if the temperature is just right, you get Life.

Of course, there's the earlier model. We call them Plants.

The basic difference between Animals and Plants is Animals are cordless, while Plants have to be plugged in.

The earlier model still had to perform the same survival tasks—eat, grow, defend, reproduce. The poor saps couldn't go anywhere, but they still solved the problem of Life.

Bruno, you may be wondering what this has to do with what you're going to say to your brother. I promise you I'm getting to it.

Years ago I took my chainsaw and cut down a great big hemlock tree. If I had cut it down for firewood or for lumber, that would have been one thing. But the truth is that I cut it down because it was blocking our view of the mountains. I'll bet it was over sixty feet tall, probably a hundred years old, and what I remember from when I cut it down is the sheer force of this toppling giant hitting the ground. The earth shook. The view improved.

But then something else.

I had taken a life.

I was a half-century old. But the tree had been standing out there in the rain and wind and sun and snow a lot longer than that. Never one peep of complaint. Never one request. Never one demand.

And the other trees around me, if they were upset they were too dignified to show it, too focused on the work of living to waste energy on me and what I'd done.

But when I let myself feel the tree hitting the ground, feel the life in this great big thing, feel the weight of what I have done, the outdoors changes.

Everything does.

It stops being me and them.

It becomes Us.

Us.

Everything that has performed the Chemical Stunt of living.

Every plant.

Every animal.

You.

Me.

Lance.

And so, Bruno, given that the universe is infinite, I would be surprised if it wasn't crawling with lots of little green stuff and tiny scurrying things. I recommend that you go to your brother Lance and say this: Maybe, bro. Maybe.

Your Fan,

Waldo Mellon

Eureka

Hey Waldo,

This chemical stunt you talk about, this thing called Life. I got a bad feeling that Life on this planet is doomed. We do things we know are destroying the house we need to live in, yet we keep doing them. I just don't get it. What's wrong with us?

Yours truly,

Confused

Dear Confused,

You're making a mistake when you call yourself Confused. You seem clear-headed about the predicament we're in. We do seem to be aiming for the bullseye of that target called Genuinely Fucked. You ask a wonderful question: What is wrong with us? I believe I have The Answer.

When I was in junior high school, the concept of the Lowest Common Denominator entered my skull. A horrible math problem containing terrifyingly huge numbers would be proposed, and then the day would be saved by that fabulous magic wand, the Lowest Common Denominator. The Lowest Common Denominator could reduce every horrifying long-winded number into an old friend—perhaps a 2, or a 3, or maybe even a refreshing 5. The only thing that changed was that the great big complicated problem became kinder.

Let's apply the principle of the Lowest Common Denominator to your question, What is wrong with us?

After many late nights in my home laboratory, I have compiled what I feel to be a complete list of human idiocies and blunders, from smoking and crucifying to ear gauges and racism. And then using my fabulous magic wand, the Lowest Common Denominator, I reduced it all into smaller, more manageable units: Laziness. Stupidity. Selfishness. Insecurity. Dishonesty. Indifference. Fear. Greed. Poverty. Misinformation. Etc., etc., etc. And then, after more months of all-nighters, sometimes drinking heavily, I arrived at what I was sure was the Very Lowest Common Denominator of Every Contemporary Problem Known to Man.

I burst out of my lab. I hollered to my colleagues—that is, to my wife and our dog and our two cats and a neighbor in the kitchen—about what I had discovered: "Survival!" I bellowed. "The Lowest Common Denominator is Survival! We do everything we do because we want to REMAIN ALIVE!"

Even the cat yawned. I raced back to my lab. Months passed. And then one morning I dashed back into the kitchen and I declared this:

WE ALL JUST WANT TO BE COMFY!
EVERYONE WHO IS COMFY
HAS TO BECOME LESS COMFY
SO THAT THOSE WHO AREN'T COMFY
CAN BE MORE COMFY!

This, I must say, was quite well received by all present and I think there is something to it.

Your Fan,
Waldo Mellon

Survival

Dear Waldo,

I know this is not the kind of question you usually answer, but would you happen to have any information concerning porcupines? My twelve-year-old has scared the wits out of his younger brothers by telling them that porcupines can shoot their quills the length of a football field. I told them it's not true, but I'm not a hundred percent sure myself.

Sincerely,
Edith from Vermont

Dear Edith from Vermont,

To answer your question, let me tell you about a date I had years ago with a Famous Beautiful Woman. I won't burden you with the details that led to this highly improbable shame-fest.

When the Famous Beautiful Woman climbed into my Jeep and went to fasten her seatbelt, I knew that the time had come for me to back out of my parking space. I had owned my Jeep for several years, so I was surprised to feel a twinge of insecurity about finding reverse.

Just to review, I glanced at the shifting diagram on top of the floor-shift knob to confirm my suspicions about what you were supposed to do when you wanted your car to go backward. That the instruction diagram appeared to me as hieroglyphs sent a heart-jolting squirt of all-purpose fight-or-flight juice into my bloodstream before I realized the knob was twisted and I was seeing it upside down.

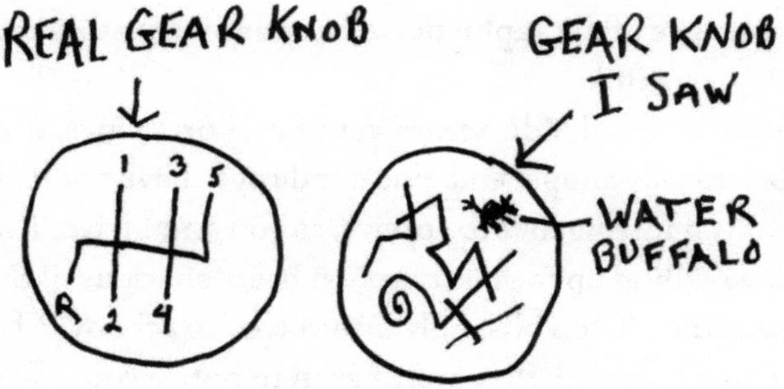

I made an instant decision to rely on instinct, threw the baby into reverse, and went forward.

After that we headed for the ocean, stopping first to get something to eat at Wendy's—her choice. We sat in a little booth, and I asked her questions about her childhood, and while she answered in complete sentences I felt like a person sinking to the bottom of the sea who is now resigned to drowning and so can focus on the small details of how death arrives, except the details of this particular death were mostly questions to myself: Don't I usually have much more saliva? Is it ketchup I like or is it mustard? Do I or do I not usually show my teeth when I smile? Could I be smelling my own feet? Where is reverse again?

And then we went to the beach where we sat on the sand and she told me about her plans to deliver a speech at the White House on the subject of something doing something bad to something else, but I was unable to distinguish nouns from verbs and then I must have driven her back to wherever back was.

All I know is that, on a very basic level, I am fond of the fellow I am, but on that particular occasion everything that I consider to be special about myself disappeared like mist into the universe and continued disappearing until the Famous Beautiful Woman got out.

Why? Because of my sophisticated Big Brain that thinks and thinks and overthinks.

On the other hand, Edith from Vermont, porcupines, thanks to their beautifully simple and efficient design, have not had to rely on evolved intelligence to survive, as you and I have. They will come waddling up to your compost heap, snack until they are full, and waddle off, too blissfully un-evolved to acknowledge the beauty of how complete they are, or even to notice you over there in the yard lying on your belly protecting your head with your hands like a marine.

They don't shoot their quills, Edith from Vermont, because they don't have to. They're absolutely fine exactly as they are. Why screw up a good thing? We, on the other hand, can find countless ways to ruin a lovely afternoon.

Your Fan,
Waldo Mellon

Forgiveness

Dear Waldo,

I have done a horrible thing. It's such a horrible thing that I can't tell anybody. I don't know what to do with this horrible thing in my head. I'm hoping you can help me.

Anonymous

Dear Anonymous,

Unless you're born and then die real quick, you will live to do what you think are horrible things. Take me, for instance.

When I was around seven, I was left alone at the house. Just me. Me and a big white bunny. I can't remember the name of the big white bunny, but I know the big white bunny belonged to my older brother Jimbo. I didn't have a bunny. I decided I wanted to play with my brother Jimbo's big white bunny.

And now I'm taking my brother Jimbo's big white bunny out of its cage and I'm throwing it up and I'm letting it land on the floor. And I'm picking it back up again and throwing it up and letting it land on the floor again. And I do it one more time before putting my brother Jimbo's big white bunny back into the cage, and off I go.

When my mom and my dad and my brothers came home somebody noticed that something was not right with my brother Jimbo's big white bunny. My brother Jimbo's big white bunny could not move its hind legs. When you picked it up its hind legs just dangled. After a few days my father got a shoebox and a rag, and he put my brother Jimbo's big white bunny into the shoebox and he poured some chloroform onto the rag and then he put the rag into the shoebox with my brother Jimbo's big white bunny and he put the top back on the box and he held it tightly, tightly until everything stopped moving.

Anonymous, we have a Public Self and we have a Private Self. They will always be two separate things. Our greatest mischief comes when we think no one is watching.

Your Private Self is your Water, the stuff you were born with.

Your Public Self is your Gumbo, the meat and potatoes and spices that your experiences have tossed into your pot.

It was my Water that tossed my brother Jimbo's bunny high into the air. Why? Who can say? Jealousy? Power? Curiosity?

It was my Gumbo that told me to tell no one.

Anonymous, did you ever have a Treasure Box when you were a kid? I did. It was a cigar box I glued crap onto in art class. At first I put into it any interesting thing I found—a butterfly wing, a heart-shaped good-luck stone, an ocean-smoothed piece of glass. But as I got older I became more selective. I put fewer things into the box because my notion of what was truly special tightened. It's my feeling that we all have a Treasure Box in our head. It's where we store our essence—our greatest pleasures, our proudest moments, memories of our loves and our greatest sorrows, fragmented gems that will not go away.

And so, Anonymous, why not place into that same Treasure Box the most horrible of our horrors? The things you want no one to know about yourself. Your weaknesses. Your insecurities. Your embarrassments. Your doubts. Your self-imposed agonies. Your useless self-loathing. That's where I decided to put the killing of my brother Jimbo's big white rabbit.

Answer honestly: Which has done a better job of sharpening your focus on the difference between Good and Bad—the Good things you have done, or the Bad things you have done?

Whatever horrible thing you did, I recommend that you try not to do that sort of thing again, and that you place it gently into your Treasure Box and then move on.

Your Fan,
Waldo Mellon

Problems

Dear Waldo,

I've writ you now I don't know how many times asking you about my jowls. How come no answer. You write back to all these other people with less important problems, so what about my jowls.

Sidney

Dear Sidney,

I apologize for not responding to your who-knows-how-many letters concerning your jowls. I'm developing some jowls as well, and I agree with you, they're not something you'd choose to have on your face. But I do not consider jowls to be a major problem. What they are is a fwapshank:

> fwapshank. (fwap'shank). *n.* A problem that disappears completely when ignored, without any negative consequences whatsoever.

Here's a short list of other popular fwapshanks:

1. Anything to do with the hair on your head
2. The inevitable physical changes of aging
3. Every bad thought about Death
4. Everything dealing with fashion

5. Scratches on new things, except eyeglasses
6. Embarrassing fruit dangling from your family tree
7. Things you said that you wish you could take back
8. Things you wish you had said but didn't
9. The size of anything on you that cannot be changed
10. Regrets

There are many, many other fwapshanks that may hound you incessantly and show up for no apparent reason. Do yourself a favor. Run this test to determine if what you are worrying about is A Real Problem or just a Fwapshank:

1. Stop thinking about it.
2. Assess whether or not your stopping thinking about it had any negative consequences.
3. If it had no negative consequences, what you got there is a fwapshank. Stop thinking about it IMMEDIATELY.

Sidney, I do know this: what you and me've got with these jowls of ours is a fwapshank. Let's move on, bud, what do you say?

Your Fan,
Waldo Mellon

Power

Dear Waldo,

I was drinking way too much and I passed out. When I woke up I was on the pavement of some parking lot somewhere and there was this bumper sticker less than two feet from my eyeballs that said "Power corrupts, and absolute power corrupts absolutely." I carry a pencil with me at all times just in case I get a great idea that could get me out of this fucking hole I'm in, and I found a bag on the ground and I wrote this power corrupts thing down because there was just something about it.

Then I got up and had the greatest time with my best friend Stevie who is sick as a dog right now and we passed out under some bridge and when I woke up I couldn't believe it. There was another one of these messages in spray paint on the cement right where I was looking that said "Youth is wasted on the young." I wrote that one down on the bag too.

Then, later, I was helping Stevie throw up and when he finished it was quiet for a while and I took out that bag and looked at those two messages. They kind of blended together in my head so I took out my pencil and wrote down what I was thinking and I showed it to Stevie. And he said, "You know what? That's the goddam truth." What I had written down was "Power is wasted on the powerful."

Power is wasted on the powerful. That's the fucking truth. Them powerful sons of bitches in charge, they don't give a fuck.

Stevie's throwing up again. If we had fucking power, he'd be in a real bed with clean sheets and there would be nurses and doctors all around him saying Stevie Stevie Stevie. But the goddam thing is, if me and Stevie had power, why the fuck would we be any different? Soon enough, we'd be the assholes. So just forget the whole fucking thing.

Fuck it.

Les

Dear Les,

Fuck it indeed. Your letter reminds me that a lisp can upend the most eloquent speaker, and that bad spelling can disguise the most electric writing, and that people who say "fuck" all the time may be easy to dismiss. It's a shame a kind heart these days isn't close to enough.

Your Fan,

Waldo Mellon

Garbage

Dear Waldo,

I was in the college library gassed out of my mind on this sick weed and I wandered up to the third floor and there was this enormous globe of the world. This globe must be like thirty feet in diameter. So I started spinning it because a sign says that's okay to do and as I kept spinning it I had this amazing thought: What if I had a giant rake, see, and I raked up all the people in the world and all the stuff all the people in the world had ever made such as houses and cities and bridges and roads and cars and furniture and trucks and garbage and bulldozers and planes and trains—I'm talking about absolutely everything that would not be on this earth if it wasn't for people—and then what if I raked all this shit into one big pile somewhere in the United States? My question to you, Waldo, is this: What's the smallest state you think I could fit that entire junk pile in? Mind-blower, yes?

Can't wait to hear your answer.

Daniel F. Twistworth

Dear Daniel,

Stoned out of your ever-loving gourd or not, I think you've stumbled upon a fascinating and revealing proposition. I'll bet most human beings think of the world as theirs, as a stage made especially for them, by them. But this giant rake concept of yours makes me realize that people, for all their huffing and puffing, have had little to do with most of what exists on our planet. Most of it has gone on without them.

In answer to your question, I'm guessing that the smallest state that could accommodate absolutely everything you've raked up is Colorado. I like it because it's a tidy rectangle that makes for a well-defined dump. I could be way off. What's your guess?

No matter what your guess is, I find it unsettling to consider that whenever that pile of stuff you've raked up greets the morning sun, that pile of shit is the biggest problem the world has. Us and our crap.

Great question, Daniel. Thank you!

Your Fan,

Waldo Mellon

Heartache

Dear Waldo,

I'm twenty-four, and everybody says I'm heartbroken, but I think it's way more than that. When J. said they were in love with someone else, it was like a bomb went off. I can't even eat. I can't even sleep. I don't want to do anything. How do I get out of this? I have to get out of this. Please help me if you can.

Heartbroken x 1000

Dear Heartbroken x 1000,

Second only to a loved one dying, what you are going through is the most unpleasant emotional experience a person can endure without bleeding.

Yes, a bomb did go off. Everything that used to give structure to your life was reshaped by this bomb into a pile of rubble.

And what hoodlum planted the bomb? Here's the great news: It wasn't your ex., that no-good bum J. No, there were two other bumbling assassins at work:

Thinking and Feeling

Working together, this tag-team duo of Thinking and Feeling can tear any life apart. And so, Heartbroken x 1000, in order to avoid this kind of mayhem in the future, let's get you better acquainted with these two mischief makers.

Thoughts are a little like hummingbirds. They dash and dart, zig and zag. Here one moment, gone the next. Only when the nectar is sweet will they stay in one place for long.

Feelings are more like whales. They glide and undulate, surface and dive. They are not eager to move on quickly.

Some Thoughts require no special attention. They pop in, they pop out. But other Thoughts set off flares that light up the night sky with wondering, and then wondering sends up more flares, and still more.

And then—uh-oh—sooner or later Feelings show up. And here's where the trouble begins. Because when Feelings enter the picture, Thinking knows it will be called upon to clean up the mess.

And this, Heartbroken x 1000, is where you are at the moment. Your Brain has delivered a bomb. The bomb has exploded. You're an emotional wreck. You rely on your Brain to come to the rescue. But with this particular mess—the losing of a partner in love—your Brain is no help.

Here's why: Your Thinking is as modern as today. It has been shaped by the culture of your lifetime. But your Feelings are as ancient as your species. They are concerned with only one thing: survival. And if you distill your relationship with J. into its evolutionary essence, what really happened is you have lost a mating partner. You may or may not have wanted to populate the planet with more of you, and having children may have been the last thing on your mind, but this is irrelevant. Because the evolutionary point of the hard and complicated and goofy work of courtship is reproduction. You're not looking for a pen pal. It's not laughs you're after. It's not someone to help you look for your phone under the couch. We are all, like it or not, still evolutionarily programmed for scouring the countryside for someone with which to do some good old-fashioned screwing. Reproducing is what our outlandishly pleasurable sexual equipment is evolutionarily sculpted to do. We want to do it even when we don't want to do it.

And so, Heartbroken x 1000, what's to be done about these two hopelessly unsuited bedfellows, Thinking and Feeling? You can try this and you can try that, but in my experience there's only one solution that has stood the test of time:

TIME

I want to rephrase that again for clarity:

TIME TIME TIME

May I repeat that in another way for emphasis:

TIME
TIME
TIME

I really hope this helps.
Your Fan,
Waldo Mellon

You

Dear Waldo,

My question is, how many different types of assholes can one human be in a single lifetime?

Thank you,

Everett

Dear Everett,

You ask a terrific question and I'm delighted to tell you that the maximum number of assholes you can be is four.

That is, everybody gets to be five Main Yous, but only four of them can be considered assholes.

Here are the Five Main Yous that everybody, and I do mean everybody, is:

1. You You
2. Agent You
3. Smart You
4. Stupid You
5. Critic You

In hopes of shedding some light on everyone's potential to be a wide variety of incredible assholes, let's look at a typical morning to see how each of the Five Yous operates.

You're sound asleep. The sound-asleep-you is your You You. Your You You may snore and fart but it is simply the husk of you, the thing you are inside of, and it cannot be considered an asshole any more than a carrot can be considered an asshole.

When you wake up in the morning, your You You is usually joined first by your Agent You. Your Agent You goes over your appointments, such as brushing teeth and getting dressed and making breakfast and so forth, but when Agent You starts talking about your job and your ambition and how terrific you could be if you only did this and if only you did that, you wish the asshole would just shut up for a couple minutes. And this will trip a little anxiety switch that will wake up the Twins—Stupid You and Smart You.

And now the squabbling begins. Agent You clearly favors Smart You over Stupid You, and this ignites a shouting match, which unfortunately wakes up Critic You. Critic You is an opinionated son of a bitch who is never happy with anything you've done, and now you haven't even shaved yet and your Four Assholes are already at each other's throats.

I must report that there is also a sixth You, but I'm sorry to say not everybody gets to have one of these. The sixth you is the Wise You. You get a Wise You only when your Smart You and your Stupid You ignore the Agent You and the Critic You and have the good fortune to really enjoy each other.

When this happens, you may pull off the miracle of loving yourself.

Thanks for your letter, Everett. Hang in there.

Your Fan,

Waldo Mellon

Kindness

Yo Asswipe,

It's me again. The harelip-one-leg-no-feet guy from way back at the beginning, remember me? I've been following this whole rap of yours, and I've had it with you and your nonsense. Since my last letter I got a eye poked out by a pool cue. With my one good eye I still get a real good look at God and the experiments this fucker is supposedly running, and this particular one here on earth is not turning out so hot. There's babies being tossed into dumpsters. There's piles of corpses everywhere. And then there's some rich chick eating fish eggs in some fancy restaurant across from some pretty boy on coke and ten feet down there's people like me shoveling their shit out of clogged sewer pipes. The fucking experiment ain't working, and yet you with two good eyes, you don't see it. Or maybe you do. Which makes you worse than blind. You are a phony. I can feel it. I can smell it. The difference is I am honest. I see that life sucks and everybody is a selfish prick, and it will be me who has the last laugh.

Last time ever,

Your Demon

Dear Demon,

Sensational letter. You are absolutely right. I am aware of horrible things. And I'm certain that the horrible things I do know about are less horrible than the horrible things I do not know about.

Agony is everywhere. But then, so are these things:

Doors held open.
The light of candles.
Tears of longing.
The holding of hands.
The scent of babies.
Crow's feet.
Any bow in any hair.
The searching for the right word.
The selecting of a hat.
The notes of that melody.
The looking-forward-to.
The right pillow.
That fantasy.
Merrying down the boulevard.
A really good potato chip.
Feeling understood.
The look in a batter's eye.
Every blush.
The clear night sky.
The struggle not to smile.
The flapping of lips.
People waving.
Bumping your head.
Giving the finger wrong.
The hiccups.
Spitting onto your own shirt.
A kiss.

Does Life care about fairness?

Not one hoot.

Does Life compensate?

Never by design.

Does Life keep score?

How could it? There's no scorekeeper.

Is the universe chaotic and uncaring?

Yes.

Is the universe mystical and miraculous?

Yes.

And I can hear you, My Demon, groaning and growling. And I don't blame you. So let's make a deal. Let's put aside the tangled trip-wires of good and bad and right and wrong and fair and unfair and what is and what isn't, and then let's run an experiment. What if the first thing you do when you wake up and you put your feet onto the earth is this: you begin each day with one tiny, quiet, shimmering goal. Your one tiny, quiet, shimmering goal is this:

Be Kind

If you don't want to do it, then don't do it. But if you're willing to do it, I'd be really grateful if you would report back to me from time to time, please. I value your feedback.

Your Fan,

Waldo Mellon

ABOUT THE AUTHOR

Waldo Mellon is the name given to Steven Saint Lawrence Adams when he was in a rock and roll band at Dartmouth College fifty years ago. Why he uses it as a pen name for this, his first book, is something he has not yet figured out. He has spent most of his life writing screenplays, three of which have been made into movies he is not particularly fond of. When he was a child his parents died and he and his three brothers were raised in the household of Jane and Kurt Vonnegut, which may or may not help to explain things.